D0559861

# Misplaced Talent

# Misplaced Talent

**A GUIDE TO MAKING BETTER PEOPLE DECISIONS**

**JOE UNGEMAH**

WILEY

Cover design: Michael J. Freeland

This book is printed on acid-free paper.

Copyright © 2015 by Joe Ungemah. All rights reserved

Published by John Wiley & Sons, Inc., Hoboken, New Jersey
Published simultaneously in Canada

No part of this publication may be reproduced, stored in a retrieval system, or transmitted in any form or by any means, electronic, mechanical, photocopying, recording, scanning, or otherwise, except as permitted under Section 107 or 108 of the 1976 United States Copyright Act, without either the prior written permission of the Publisher, or authorization through payment of the appropriate per-copy fee to the Copyright Clearance Center, 222 Rosewood Drive, Danvers, MA 01923, (978) 750-8400, fax (978) 646-8600, or on the web at www.copyright.com. Requests to the Publisher for permission should be addressed to the Permissions Department, John Wiley & Sons, Inc., 111 River Street, Hoboken, NJ 07030, (201) 748-6011, fax (201) 748-6008, or online at www.wiley.com/go/permissions.

Limit of Liability/Disclaimer of Warranty: While the publisher and author have used their best efforts in preparing this book, they make no representations or warranties with the respect to the accuracy or completeness of the contents of this book and specifically disclaim any implied warranties of merchantability or fitness for a particular purpose. No warranty may be created or extended by sales representatives or written sales materials. The advice and strategies contained herein may not be suitable for your situation. You should consult with a professional where appropriate. Neither the publisher nor the author shall be liable for damages arising herefrom.

For general information about our other products and services, please contact our Customer Care Department within the United States at (800) 762-2974, outside the United States at (317) 572-3993 or fax (317) 572-4002.

Wiley publishes in a variety of print and electronic formats and by print-on-demand. Some material included with standard print versions of this book may not be included in e-books or in print-on-demand. If this book refers to media such as a CD or DVD that is not included in the version you purchased, you may download this material at http://booksupport.wiley.com. For more information about Wiley products, visit www.wiley.com.

*Library of Congress Cataloging-in-Publication Data:*

Ungemah, Joe.

  Misplaced talent : a guide to making better people decisions / Joe Ungemah.
    pages cm
  Includes index.
   ISBN 978-1-119-03094-2 (hardback); ISBN 978-1-119-03097-3 (pdf);
   ISBN 978-1-119-03090-4 (epub)
  1. Decision making.  2. Personnel management.   I. Title.
   HD30.23.U54 2015
   658.3′128—dc23

                                          2015008302

Printed in the United States of America

10  9  8  7  6  5  4  3  2  1

# Contents

# List of Figures

# Foreword

When Joe asked me to write a foreword for his book, *Misplaced Talent*, the request arrived on the very same day that I completed an article I was working on with a colleague from another university looking at the relationship between science and practice ("the science-practice gap"). We reported on some research we had been doing on the ways in which practitioners bring scientific evidence to bear in their practice within the field of "occupational psychology," as we Brits call it, or, for those with a more European or North American background, work or industrial-organizational psychology.

Despite differences in name, what comes through from the wealth of international experience upon which this book is based is that there are many more commonalities than differences when we look at how psychology has been applied to the world of work across the globe, but yet practitioners can sometimes struggle in their attempts to translate and apply to their own practice the very rich body of scientific research and theory upon which the profession is based. This is why *Misplaced Talent* is such a useful book.

Recognizing that the fundamental drivers of performance in the workplace stem directly from the most basic and deeply held set of motivations and desires that we all share in common as members of the human race, Joe's ability to see beyond the surface details, through to the very heart of what drives human beings in a work context, and then to use the insights thus gained to see the bigger organizational picture is what characterizes both his own work as a practitioner and this book.

I recall a time over a decade ago when I invited Joe to make a presentation at the university research centre I was running at the time. Duly armed with enough data to satisfy the hardest-nosed of empiricists, along with a PowerPoint presentation of accompanying statistical analyses that would leave even the most eager of statisticians similarly sated, he scrolled effortlessly through his slides, pointing out the key findings to the varied audience of economists, sociologists, psychologists, and other assorted disciplinary specialists that are to be found in most university-based business schools.

After the presentation, the usual round of questions and answers began, whereupon, of course, I expected the conventional criticisms to emerge—the sociologists taking one point of view, the economists another, and so forth. Instead, I was surprised that, although each group had a range of challenging and probing questions, they all seemed to agree on the main points that he had managed to distill from the data.

In *Misplaced Talent*, Joe achieves a similar effect—firmly evidence-based and drawing from well-established research findings while at the same time highlighting the key points that are most useful for practitioners when considering how to apply these ideas to the particular talent management issues they are facing. His book is very clearly a product of his own personal embodiment of the scientist-practitioner model to which all work and organizational psychologists aspire.

The scientist-practitioner model, which emphasizes both methodological rigor and also relevance to the reality of work organizations, on the other, reflects what has been termed the "rigor-relevance debate. According to this debate, the research-practice gap arises through academics engaging too often in what has been termed "pedantic science" (obsessed with meticulous theoretical and methodological precision, but of little practical value or relevance to those working in organizations) and practitioners sometimes resorting to popularist science, based more on commercial interests and client acceptability than sound scientific research.

A similar debate on the relationship between science and practice has taken place within the field of management more widely. Denise Rousseau, in her presidential address to the Academy of Management, called for practitioners to adopt an evidence-based approach, defining evidence-based management as "translating principles based on best evidence into organizational practices" and positioning the approach as a response to the research-practice gap that was bemoaned by both scholars and practitioners. Both seemed to acknowledge that management practice was often, if not usually, based on something other than the best available scientific evidence—a suspicion supported by research indicating that less 1 percent of HR managers regularly read the academic literature. It is for this reason that *Misplaced Talent* is such a timely and useful book.

Based on sound evidence, but at the same time questioning the suitability of some tried-and-tested approaches within their contexts of application, the book advances practice-based knowledge by drawing key lessons from the academic literature and scrutinizing the ways in which they have been applied or, on occasion, misapplied in practice. A key feature is how these have been summarized into practical, useful pointers for practitioners, illustrating relevant issues and dilemmas through copious examples from the author's own practice that bring to life the challenges facing practitioners in the contemporary, fast-changing workplace.

The picture emerging from our work at the Centre for Progressive Leadership of the role that business leaders and top talent of the future will play in this changing landscape is very different from the one played out in organizations today. We live in exciting times, and the increasingly networked context in which organizations find themselves means that their scope will only become wider as complex networks of suppliers, partners, customers, and other stakeholders emerge and interact in increasingly sophisticated and unpredictable ways.

Those at the top of the organization will, as I have argued elsewhere, need to become both "business model innovators" and "social facilitators," while the way in which roles are continually reconfigured will present a challenge to those lower down in the hierarchy, even as those hierarchies themselves shift their shapes.

Those charged with matching people to these new roles must align a more diverse set of people through networks of "open innovation" and, while we cannot predict exactly how the story will unfold, the only certainty is that the organizations of tomorrow will be radically different from those of today in ways that we have yet to imagine. *Misplaced Talent* provides a valuable resource for any practitioners faced with the immense challenge of responding to these trends as they negotiate their way through this rapidly changing backdrop to develop the dynamic capabilities upon which the organizations of the future will depend.

One of the central themes of the book is person-environment fit (P-E fit), which is often misunderstood as being concerned simply with the degree of match (or mismatch) between a person and his or her environment. This is structural and static, whereas a more transactional framework has the potential to be process-oriented, taking account of the dynamic nature of the relationship between the person and the environment as the individual engages in "commerce" with that environment.

Such a conceptualization engenders a systems view of people at work, with each component of the system being dependent upon the others. The adoption of a P-E fit perspective presents a challenge to both the practitioner and researcher. Compromises will have to be made in the short term, as currently available tools and techniques account for only a static perspective. While the profession of occupational psychology may be some way off from realizing the full potential of P-E fit, it does at least now have somewhere to begin in *Misplaced Talent*.

The book represents both a valuable resource for the practitioner and a forward-thinking contribution to the profession as a whole as it begins rising to the challenge of a greater understanding of how an individual's personal values, goals, and commitments express what is important to him or her in particular transactions with the work environment and what this, in turn, means for him or her personally, in terms of their significance for the values and beliefs that are held dear.

In this sense, then, Joe offers the reader a chance to consider how people's personal characteristics and belief systems act as a "perceptual lens" that enables them to create meaning out of their work lives. This focus on individual subjectivity and personal meaning goes some way toward providing a foundation for a fuller understanding of how people perform at their best at work, based on a genuinely cognitive-phenomenological account of human functioning.

The book provides readers with an opportunity to consider how well they understand the drives and desires of those around them, and also invites a critical evaluation of how work is designed and how they select and develop those who do it.

*Professor Dean Bartlett, Ph.D., C.Psychol., FHEA, AFBPsS, HCPC, Registered Occupational Psychologist*
*London, April 2015*

# Preface

I spend the better part of my day helping organizations make better people decisions. From redesigning a recruitment process, to running focus groups with leaders to define what good talent looks like or facilitating individual and group development, I am on the front line, working directly with leaders and professional talent managers to improve how their organizations are attracting and retaining the best workers.

What has spurred me to write this book is a feeling that the tools and processes that I help set in motion swim against the tide of how organizations naturally operate. Tendencies like hiring the candidate who feels right or arguing that a department really is not like any other in the company (and, therefore, common job definitions don't apply) undermine the architecture that I put in place.

This had led me to question the work that I do. Are the tools and techniques that I promote really cut out for the job? Are there better ways to manage talent than what is accepted as common practice? Is the support that I typically offer inadequate to ensure long-term change?

I have concluded that there is plenty of scope to improve how organizations make people decisions. I believe we are in a state of *misplaced talent*. At times, we park our best and brightest staff in the wrong places, where they are either not maximizing what they can do or become at risk of drifting away due to lack of interest in the job. At other times, we can forget what really matters to the organization, placing too much emphasis on jobs and functions that have minimal impact on what a company is tasked to do. And still other times, we bet on the wrong talent to lead and grow our businesses, overlooking employees or applicants who are more deserving and capable.

By taking a step back, questioning what works, and becoming better advocates, we can make headway against bad practice. This book will help us do that. It is intended for anyone responsible for making people decisions in the workplace. Whether you work in an advisory capacity or as a people leader with full responsibility for your staffing decisions, the topics discussed in this book will have relevance for you. I use the term "practitioner" liberally, to designate any individual who is involved in advising or making people decisions.

If, like me, you work in an advisory capacity, we have an obligation to promote the benefit of tools and techniques that are known to improve people decisions in the organizations we are servicing. Our job is to steer organizational leaders toward proven techniques and away from pseudo-science, while balancing needs for cost-effectiveness and efficiency.

Leaders, too, have an obligation to ensure that they are valuing people decisions as highly as the other decisions they make. If leaders uniformly spent the same amount of time and energy on people decisions as they do on strategy or finance, I believe that organizations would look and feel very different than they do today.

When it comes to the techniques that constitute good people practice, not much has changed in recent history. Competency design, assessment to inform hiring, and psychometric-led development are used as much today as they were five decades ago. Online technology may have increased tool accessibility and speed, but fundamentally, the job of a practitioner still involves conducting job analysis, recruiting talent, assessing capability and motivation, developing staff, and implementing change programs.

What *has* changed is the desire and ability for organizations to question the return on investment that their people practices have on improved business efficiency, staff engagement, and performance. Like never before, organizations have at their disposal vast amounts of data on employees, customers, and financial indicators that can and are being used to validate whether people practices are adding value to the business. Coupled with a continuing need to save cost following the recent recession, only those programs that are able to prove their value are spared.

A storm is brewing. On one hand, organizations are expecting more from us as practitioners, to demonstrate the value of what we bring to the business. Yet on the other hand, people decisions are routinely made without the rigor and discipline they deserve. I believe that now is the time to take a hard look at the tools and techniques we employ and determine which ones have the right to be widely adopted in our organizations. Only then can we engage businesses about the value we bring them through improved people decisions.

In this book, I will take us on a tour of current people practices. This book diverges from an academic discourse on talent management by focusing on what those of us on the front line witness and advise our clients to adopt. I will lay on the line the potential benefits and drawbacks of various approaches, sometimes arguing that specific tools and techniques do more harm than good and should therefore be abandoned. More often, I will demonstrate that the tools and techniques are sound, but the ways in which they are applied are in drastic need of improvement. I passionately believe that there is an incredible amount of potential to improve the lives of employees and the organizations they work for, if we can focus our efforts on the right set of practices.

We will know that we have succeeded as practitioners when the employment relationship leaders share with their employees has improved. Like any other social relationship, both parties need to feel fulfilled and trust that they are moving in a common direction. The decisions leaders make about recruitment, assignment of work responsibilities, staff recognition, and discipline (among others) act either toward or against a strong employment relationship. We as practitioners can ensure that the best decisions are made by putting in place structures and techniques that heighten the quality and transparency of the information guiding their judgment.

The term *person-environment fit* has been coined to express the quality of the employment relationship. The fit between an employee and his or her workplace is said to be high when three conditions are met. First, organizations effectively apply the knowledge, skills, and abilities of employees to accomplish job tasks. Second, organizations fulfill the tangible and intangible needs of their staff. Third, employees feel that their efforts are coordinated and contributing toward a common purpose. A fuller account of the person-environment model is presented later in the book. For now, these three tenets provide an underlying structure to the book that will aid us in evaluating the contribution different techniques make.

In Chapter 1, we will look at how organizations identify and structure their expectations of staff performance and the type of workplace they cultivate. The discussion begins by reviewing the origins of job analysis, as characterized by Taylorism and the Human Relations Movement, followed by the arrival of competencies as the primary vehicle organizations use to set a benchmark for people decisions. I will argue that frameworks often fall short in delivering useful guidance, with content that is heavily slanted toward behaviors (ignoring skills or experience) and too generic in terminology (glossing over functional differences), resulting in employees focusing energy in the wrong places.

With the criteria set for what type of talent organizations are looking for, attention turns toward finding the talent that will meet these needs. Chapter 2 explores what companies are doing to promote an appealing "employer brand," how they define an "employer value proposition," and source the best possible talent available. Although some companies have a clear and effective strategy about how to attain top talent, more common are haphazard campaigns based on limited insight about what an employer can bring its staff. Offering the wrong type of incentives or over-promising on commitments makes for an unstable employment relationship.

Chapter 3 unpacks the first tenet of person-environment fit, specifically that organizations effectively apply the knowledge, skills, and abilities of their employees. We will look at the tools and techniques practitioners employ to identify the capabilities of staff, including ability tests, interviews, and job simulations. By using the criteria of reliability and validity as our guide, I will argue that more can be done to correctly identify the best candidate for the job.

Focus turns to the fulfillment of employee needs (the second tenet of person-environment fit) in Chapter 4. Practitioners today use a variety of psychometrics to identify the personality characteristics, motivators, and values of current and future employees. However, the quality and relevance of these tools vary greatly and, therefore, have the potential to misrepresent what an employee desires from his or her workplace. Without validation and exploration of what could be reasonably accommodated, too much is assumed about what drives and engages talent.

The last tenet of person-environment fit, where both parties feel that they are moving in the same direction, will be discussed in Chapter 5. The chapter introduces the term *psychological contract*, which represents the glue that binds employees to their workplace.

We will investigate the various ways practitioners attempt to invest in the psychological contract, including raising self-awareness, coaching and mentoring, skills training and certification, and job rotations. I will argue that so-called development programs are often assessments in disguise, whereby the information gained about employees' weaknesses can be used against them in future promotion decisions or job reassignments. Moreover, development has a tendency to focus on a narrow set of organizational priorities, which effectively build skills, but do little to improve the psychological contract and keep employees engaged in the long term.

In Chapter 6, we will look at what practitioners do to repair a broken psychological contract. There are many causes for a breakdown. For example, economic challenges can make for a more stressful workplace environment. Alternatively, the favoritism shown to employees engaged in *high potential programs* can cause a rift with those not selected for the program. Employees, too, can be at fault in breaking the psychological contract by failing to perform well in their jobs. Practitioners attempt to remedy breakdowns in the psychological contract by redeploying staff, preparing for change through succession planning, and introducing performance management systems. Yet, many of these initiatives fundamentally change the psychological contract from a relational to a transactional type, which can snowball into further breakdown and only works to prolong the inevitable loss of talent from the organization.

Each of the chapters is written in a way that allows you to dip in and out of the book, depending on what types of people decisions are of most relevance and interest to you. A table of contents by topic is presented for quick reference. I hope that this book challenges you to consider for yourself which practices will make for better people decisions in your own workplace. With a little luck and diligence, we might be able to declare that we have successfully found the best talent for our organizations, deployed them in the right places, and kept them very happy and productive. At least, this should be our ambition.

# Chapter 1

## Frameworks

Without having job criteria in place, there is simply no way of predicting with any degree of confidence whether your people decisions are fair and rational. Practitioners rely on job descriptions and talent management frameworks to combat the risks of poor people decisions, because when you start racking up all the direct and indirect costs of an unfilled vacancy or a poorly placed new hire, the costs are striking, especially for roles that are core to the business.

One of my clients put its business analytics team to the task of figuring out how much it costs to replace a front-line employee. These are not high level positions, but rather staff working in retail branches and call centers. By the time the analyst calculated the cost of advertisement, the time spent by the recruitment team to screen and interview candidates, the loss of productivity because the role was vacant, and the cost to induct a new employee, the total figure was a staggering $57,000 per vacancy.

You might be skeptical and think this sounds too high, but even if you accept that the cost is only half as high, the damage of hiring the wrong people or failing to address engagement issues are substantial. When you consider that an annual turnover rate of 30 percent is the norm for certain industries, a modest improvement in retention (i.e., people staying on for a few extra months on average) can save a large organization millions of dollars and potentially gain a few customers along the way, through a more positive customer experience with an engaged company representative.

Before employees can be hired or money spent on development, practitioners must establish criteria about what they are trying to accomplish. For recruitment, identifying critical skills and experiences ensure that they hire the candidate most likely to perform well on the job. For development, understanding what needs to be improved and for what reason can ensure that training budgets are invested wisely.

This chapter is devoted to exploring the frameworks put in place by practitioners to help guide people decisions throughout their organization. By defining what the employee and organization, respectively, bring to the table, as well as the glue that holds them together, it is hoped that decisions can be made by their collective ability to strengthen the employment relationship.

The chapter begins by charting the origins of job analysis and the subsequent change in emphasis from the division of labor to the drivers of employee performance, followed by the rise of behavioral competencies as the language practitioners use to define the workplace. We will then look at the complexities of defining a structure that works effectively across levels, functions, and jobs, as well as two of the common applications for talent management frameworks in recruitment and development.

I aim to demonstrate that there exists an inherent tradeoff between defining a framework that accounts for the intricacies between jobs and its usefulness for making sound talent management decisions. The role of the practitioner is to use his or her best judgment in weighing the pros and cons of each alternative, settling on the framework that will have maximum utility for the organization at this specific point in time. Right now, I believe that the pendulum has swung too far, with frameworks accounting for only a fraction of the employment relationship (focusing excessively on behaviors) and applying generic language across highly divergent roles. Together, these trends provide practitioners with the greatest opportunity to help their organizations reframe what top talent looks like.

## Origins of Job Analysis

Modern day practitioners are not the first to be interested in the content and structure of jobs. The origins of job analysis are evident with the development of more complex and interdependent civilizations. For example, Imperial China had a long-standing tradition of regularly testing the worthiness of government officials. In 1115 BCE, six skill sets were defined as part of this testing regime, specifically writing, arithmetic, music, archery, horsemanship, and ceremonies and rites. As a second example from the other side of the world, Socrates in the 5th century BCE mused about the allocation of work in his description of the ideal state.

The first major work that can be considered a precursor to job analysis was completed in 1747. Diderot, busily writing his encyclopedia, was so disturbed by the lack of clarity around how jobs were defined in the trades, arts, and crafts that he took it upon himself to create a job classification system. Diderot kicked off a trend that would continue in France for nearly a century. Between 1780 and 1830, France defined an encyclopedia of occupations and the basic qualifications required for civil service, implementing bureau examinations to select the most suitable candidates. The British Empire was quick to follow, similarly focused on the civil service and the challenge of effectively managing colonies located around the world.

The late 19th century witnessed reform in the United States, initiated by Lincoln voicing his displeasure at the "inefficient and wasteful results of political appointments." A firm tradition of assessing abilities and skills was thus established. The full potential of job analysis was not realized until it was applied beyond the civil service, coinciding with the establishment of Industrial Psychology as something different than other psychological disciplines. Early pioneers include Frederick Taylor, who relied on job analysis to fuel his principles of Scientific Management; Hugo Munsterberg and his quest to identify worker characteristics that would result in greater job fit; and Frank and Lillian Gilbreth with their development of time and motion studies (see Figure 1.1).

A huge amount of momentum for job analysis was gained as an outcome of the First World War. The U.S. Army was keen to improve how soldiers were selected and placed into service (Figure 1.2). When the Great Depression hit, attention turned to utilizing worker abilities and getting the great masses of civilians back to work. The Social Science Research Council and the National Research Council sought to utilize job analysis to identify the core characteristics of jobs and how they differ by vocation. This work led the U.S. Employment Service to establish the Occupational Research Program in 1934, which sought to draft a Dictionary of Occupational Titles

FIGURE 1.1 Image from Frank and Lillian Gilbreth's 1918 Ball Brothers Mason Jar Study That Targeted How to Improve Worker Efficiency by Reducing Motion

(DOT) and create a taxonomy of worker characteristics that could be used to select candidates. The program resulted in a taxonomy of forty-five characteristics used by states to hire and relocate staff, with the DOT itself published in 1939.

Although interest in job analysis has remained steady, especially in light of Equal Employment Opportunity legislation, a major overhaul of the DOT did not occur until 1995, with the creation of O*Net. A consortium of prominent psychologists was hired by the U.S. Department of Labor to replace the DOT with a new classification of jobs that were representative of the U.S. economy. In addition to basic labor market information, O*Net provides a breakdown of each job by four categories.

- ◆ *Worker Characteristics:* **Abilities**, **Interests**, **Values**, and **Styles** held by the employee that are considered enduring and likely to influence their performance and acquisition of skills.

Figure 1.2 Image of U.S. Army Air Corps Cadets in 1942 Taking a Group Test to Help Determine Their Proficiency as Pilots, Navigators, or Bombardiers

- ◆ *Worker Requirements:* **Skills**, **Knowledge**, and **Education** that are gained by the employee by either doing their jobs or in preparing for a career.
- ◆ *Occupational Requirements:* **Tasks** required by the employee and the **Tools and Technology** that he or she will likely utilize on the job.
- ◆ *Occupation-Specific Information:* **Work Activities** describing the behaviors expected from employees and the **Work Context** (aka environment) that they are likely to experience.

O*Net was an ambitious project and the final product contains 571 job elements across 821 detailed occupations. Such an array of job elements provides a mindboggling number of potential combinations, and practitioners are well aware of the value O*Net brings to their toolbox.

I have had the pleasure of working alongside one of the creators of O*Net. Wally Borman is an expert practitioner, having a résumé that would make anybody deeply envious. Wally is the "chief scientist" at PDRI, as well as a professor of IO psychology at the University of South Florida. He has penned over 350 publications, served as president for the Society for Industrial and Organizational Psychology, edited four professional journals, and above all, is one of the most genuine and supportive people I have worked with.

When writing this chapter, I arranged some time to speak with Wally about the creation of O*Net and what it strove to achieve. According to Wally, the motivation for O*Net was to get beyond the DOT, which had a clumsy underlying framework that failed to provide a true comparison between jobs and did little beyond providing generic job descriptions. True comparison between jobs, with rich and thorough taxonomy, was beyond the DOT and required a major rework.

To create the content used across *worker characteristics, worker requirements, occupational requirements,* and *occupation-specific information*, the O*Net designers relied on a combination of existing theory, logic, and their extensive practical experience working in the field performing job analysis. For example, O*Net's taxonomy for *work styles* is based on the Big 5 personality model, which is the most highly researched and validated personality structure available today. Moreover, Wally was keen to point out that O*Net has a hierarchical structure that extends beyond the categorization of jobs. The hierarchy applies at a lower level to the *work activities* that drive these distinctions, accomplished by looking at differences among task complexity, importance, and frequency.

According to Wally, the greatest challenge in creating O*Net was not in drafting the content, but in gaining enough data to validate what was written. Realizing how enormous the task was of surveying job incumbents from each of the 821 jobs included in O*Net, the designers decided instead to opt for a practical approach. The designers targeted eighty jobs, which, surprisingly, made up 80 to 90 percent of people employed in the U.S. economy at the time. The design team went out to organizations with significant populations of employees working in these occupations and was warmly welcomed.

But the designers hit a roadblock. Despite a resounding initial interest from employers to participate, the response rate was shockingly poor, and solid data was captured for only thirty-five of the jobs. The design team went to Plan C and used other industrial psychologists to validate O*Net's content. This is a lesson for any practitioner working on a large scale job analysis project. Gaining commitment from job incumbents or subject matter experts is usually not a problem until they see the full extent of what is asked of them.

With the content validated to the highest practical degree, O*Net provides a solid foundation for a range of talent management activities. Wally points out its usefulness in providing criteria for recruitment or reward decisions, identifying training requirements, guiding the redeployment of staff, and informing career guidance. As an area of future application, Wally believes that O*Net could be used to inform what types of reasonable accommodation could be made for people with disabilities. But for this to occur, he believes that O*Net requires even more granular content and extensive validation with job incumbents.

Unless your day job looks like mine, you are probably wondering why anyone would ever need to do job analysis again. It appears that O*Net has done it all. O*Net has a robust content model, applies to every conceivable role in the U.S. economy (which translates well to an international context), has been validated, and, best of all, is free to use courtesy of the U.S. Department of Labor (a link is provided in the notes section of this book).

Yet, for all these advantages, O*Net does not provide a total solution. The language used in O*Net is necessarily generic and therefore cannot account for how a given occupation is interpreted by each organization. One of the popular statistics HR professionals quote is a finding that it takes six to eight months for the average employee to become fully competent in his or her role. Assuming that a suitably qualified candidate was chosen (having the skills and experiences that would be listed on O*Net), then it is not too much of a stretch to imagine that the six to eight months a new employee requires is due to the way job roles are interpreted and connected to work within a specific organization.

Bottom line, job analysis is required to capture all the idiosyncrasies that fall between the cracks of the generic job descriptions. What makes Microsoft different from Apple or Coca-Cola different from Pepsi has a lot to do with the mix of talent they have working in their organizations and the processes that they have defined for how individuals work together. Competitive advantage from a people perspective is having insight into what makes your culture, processes, and roles different from those of your rivals and then finding and nurturing the talent according to what you find. It all depends on job analysis.

## The Art and Science of Job Analysis

To conduct a job analysis, practitioners are tasked with defining the essence of a job, accomplished through interviews, focus groups, questionnaires, observation, or existing knowledge. This information is bundled together into a snapshot of a job that represents what employees are doing at that particular moment in time. As a job adapts and changes to new ways of working or different end products, the onus is on the practitioner to revise the job description. The reality is far from ideal, and I will talk more about this in a few minutes.

Below, I will present eight popular ways of conducting a job analysis. Each employs a slightly different way at gaining relevant information and, as a result, yields different information about tasks, behaviors, or personal attributes. No matter which combination of techniques is chosen, a successful job analysis is systematic (having a predefined objective and structure), comprehensive (gaining multiple, relevant viewpoints that represent the job), and timely (before any major staffing decisions are made). When done right, job analysis forms the basis for selection, appraisal, compensation, and development activities, as well as compliance with fairness legislation. Here are the main techniques trained practitioners utilize.

### Work Logs

Job incumbents are asked to keep a written record of the work they accomplish, either after a specified period of time (e.g., hourly or daily) or when they switch between tasks. Individual accounts of the workday are compiled across job incumbents to discover the key activities that make up a particular job.

### Structured Observation

A trained observer watches job incumbents fulfill their work throughout the day, using a checklist of tasks as a reference. The observer keeps track of the frequency of tasks, duration, and accuracy of the items included in the checklist. The observer will often ask questions of the job incumbent about what he or she is doing, how he or she is doing it, and why it has to be done in order to fully capture key activities and necessary behaviors.

### JOB SAMPLE

Trained observers take on the job for a set period of time. Through their experience, they take note of how they use their time, the tasks they are asked to accomplish, the approach they take in fulfilling tasks, and the required skills they should have to effectively accomplish their work. This technique is more appropriate for jobs that can be learned quickly or that take advantage of transferrable skills.

### HIERARCHICAL TASK ANALYSIS

This technique involves breaking a job down into the typical tasks performed and then breaking these down into subtasks, usually through an interview with job incumbents or a line manager. The technique elicits information around the key objectives of a job and the skills and abilities that employees should have to fulfill them.

### REPERTORY GRID

In this technique, a line manager is interviewed and presented with a series of staff comparisons. With each comparison, the manager is asked to differentiate how two staff members are different from a third staff member in their effectiveness in performing the job. The technique can elicit a broad range of content, from how someone treats colleagues or customers to the skills he or she brings to the workplace. In my experience, coordinating the range of comparisons (to ensure a range of unique combinations) and explaining the task to the manager makes this technique impractical.

### CRITICAL INCIDENT

Job incumbents or managers are interviewed and asked for examples of critical situations that involved the target job. An example could involve the winning of a key account, prevention of a major catastrophe, or major change in a business process. The interviewer explores the incident from multiple vantage points, asking how the job incumbent solved the situation, the skills or experiences that enabled her and what could have been done differently.

## CARD SORT

Using a predefined competency framework (either generic or specific to the organization), job incumbents or managers are asked to select the core competencies required for a job. I typically ask for four essential competencies and two desired competencies. Once these are selected, follow-up questions are used to reveal the rationale for each selection. By compiling results from multiple card sorts, trends in competencies can be discovered.

## VISIONARY INTERVIEW

Unlike the other interview types described above, this technique focuses on the future of a job. Senior leaders or others who have deep insight on the organization are asked about how the target job is likely to change in the medium to long term, with the aim of eliciting a list of behaviors, skills, experience, and motivations that should be prioritized now to future-proof any talent management strategy. These techniques are summarized in Figure 1.3.

When bundling job descriptions, practitioners should establish and maintain a model that will work well within their organization. Having a common job template drives consistency and allows for comparison or links across jobs. One such model could be the categories used in O*Net. Although this is a fine model to employ, I have found that the majority of clients prefer a simpler model that focuses squarely on the individual tasked with doing the job (not so much

| Direct Experience | • Job Sample |
| | • Structured Observation |
| Via Job Incumbent | • Work Logs |
| | • Critical Incident |
| | • Card Sort |
| Via Line Manager | • Hierarchical Task Analysis |
| | • Repertory Grid |
| | • Visionary Interview |

FIGURE **1.3**  Summary of Job Analysis Techniques by Source of Information

the organizational context). In my client interactions, I commonly refer to the five key ingredients of any job, which are not so different from the categories used by other consultants:

- ◆ *Key Activities:* What the individual is typically tasked to do.
- ◆ *Behavioral Competencies:* How effective job incumbents go about the job.
- ◆ *Skills:* The education and training that enable job performance.
- ◆ *Experience:* Knowledge gained in a given context that can be applied to the job.
- ◆ *Motivation:* Employee needs and preferences that require fulfillment.

The best job descriptions are focused and concise. Practitioners and line managers have a tendency to create a laundry list of character-istics across these five key ingredients. They want a little of everything, and by the time they are done, they have described a superhuman and written a document that is totally useless for selection and develop-ment decisions.

When writing a job description, I challenge my clients to hone in on no more than six absolutely essential points to include for each key ingredient. Next, I have them describe with as much precision as possible what is meant by that characteristic, to give direction to those responsible for talent management decisions. For example, if I were creating a job description for my favorite coffee shop barista, I might include the following for one of the key activities:

*Key Activity of Pulling Shots*
*Prepares to pull shots of espresso by using the portioned amount of coffee from the grinder, tamping the grounds flat, and insert-ing the filter handle into the group head. Pulls each espresso shot for approximately twenty to twenty-six seconds, watching to see that a rust colored Crema has been produced. Empties the filter handle of the used grinds, wipes clean with a towel, and purges the machine.*

What you'll notice is that this description captures the essence of the activity from beginning to end, using the actual names of the equipment being used. This level of description would be absolutely the same if I went on to describe the behaviors, skills, experience, and motivation characteristics included in the job description.

The reality is that most job descriptions I come across suffer from three fatal flaws. I have already mentioned the first, that job descriptions must be focused. Including too many characteristics waters down the effectiveness of the document for identifying candidates who have the greatest fit, as well as which skills and experiences should be nurtured by on-the-job development. Moreover, a lack of focus could interfere with the legal defensibility of decisions, by pulling attention away from critical characteristics onto those with anecdotal attachment to the job.

Second, the language of many job descriptions is so vague that it renders the document useless. It is no longer surprising to me just how many job descriptions still use phrases like *talented*, *team player*, or *self-starter*. It goes without saying that employers want a candidate who can do the job, get along with other people, and strive to achieve goals. To me, generic phrases like these are a warning that the person who wrote the job description has limited knowledge about the job or has not taken the time to commit his or her thoughts to paper.

Third, job descriptions start aging the moment they are drafted. As market conditions, technology, work processes, and organizational structures change, so does the content underlying the job description. Often job descriptions are not updated until absolutely necessary, when some major talent management decision is made. I witnessed this first hand during the economic downturn experienced in Ireland. Many of the organizations I encountered had not revised their job descriptions for years, as they had become accustomed to the Celtic Tiger years when any warm body would do. When faced with a decision about who to cut (in some cases, literally half the workforce was made redundant), they had nothing to stand on. These organizations lost precious time creating legally defensible job descriptions and assessment processes, before they could begin reacting to the downturn.

Conducting job analysis and drafting job descriptions is time-consuming and extremely repetitive work. It is, thus, not surprising that employers settle for unfocused, vague, and outdated job descriptions to guide their people decisions. Practitioners tend to under-appreciate the power of getting this right, not only for creating a standard for key talent management decisions, but for engaging business leaders in people decisions by asking for their expert opinions.

There is an alternative. Instead of looking at all five key ingredients, many practitioners advocate for drafting a competency model that applies across roles and drives the majority of talent management decisions. As will be discussed shortly, competencies can still be unfocused, vague, and outdated, and, in many ways, a competency approach makes matters worse by discounting the depth of understanding gained by using the full five key ingredients. What is captured at the individual job level will differ significantly from the group or organizational level, similar to the level of detail captured by a handheld camera compared to a satellite in space.

## Behavioral Simplicity

The definition of a competency is hard to nail down, as each organization and practitioner interprets the idea in a slightly different way. Some practitioners use competency frameworks to communicate the core mission of their organization to both job candidates and incumbents, aiming for a common way of working and a guide that can be used by managers to set priorities. Other practitioners are not so concerned with such lofty goals, but rather latch onto competency frameworks as a means of aligning human resource activities, ensuring that the criteria used for hiring are linked to development and performance management.

Because competencies serve many masters, there is a great deal of ambiguity about their definition, which is not helpful if you are a practitioner and trying to convince business leaders that they need a framework. This ambiguity is apparent in an early definition by Boyatzis (1982), who states, "A job competency is an underlying characteristic of a person which results in an effective and/or superior performance of a job . . . it may be a trait, motive, skill, aspect of one' s self image or social role, or body of knowledge that he or she uses." As long as some personal characteristic is thought to drive performance, it appears to be fair game for inclusion using this definition.

Some practitioners believe that this ambiguity is a good thing, as it allows companies to make competencies their own. If business leaders call for the role-modeling of new or different types of behavior, perhaps the competency framework should take an aspirational tone or profess some unifying values. Alternatively, high tech IT or engineering companies may want to emphasize technical achievement and, therefore, knowledge and skills could take priority in their framework.

Other practitioners don't like this. They argue that frameworks should be robust and legally defensible, especially if they are used for important people decisions around hiring, promotion, or pay. Emphasis should be on what is critical for the organization to accomplish its work. A great example for the need for rigor was a religious organization I worked with in the UK. Within their framework was the competency of "holiness." Highly relevant for their work, but hardly defensible if used to make a hiring decision. Exactly how would you evaluate how "holy" someone was?

To minimize confusion about what should be in a competency framework, practitioners commonly differentiate between two types of competencies, either behavioral or technically based. Woodruffe (1992) focuses on behavior when defining a competency as "the set of behavior patterns that the incumbent needs to bring to a position in order to perform tasks and functions with competence." Still present in this definition is a link to job performance, but absence is talk about knowledge, skills, or abilities. I'll come back to these at the end of the section. For now, I want to talk more about behaviors, as they make up the lion's share of competency frameworks.

A benchmarking survey conducted in 2006 found that behavioral competencies are well embedded in UK companies (we can assume similar take up in other geographic locations), with applications across a wide variety of people decisions. For selection, 59 percent of companies reported using their framework for sifting job candidates, while 68 percent asked competency-based interview questions. In managing existing employees, 77 percent of companies used behavioral competencies within their appraisal systems and 58 percent used competency performance to inform promotion decisions. The greatest use of competencies was in development, with 82 percent of companies using their framework to inform training content.

A well-articulated competency has three components. The first component is a short and punchy title that captures in a few words the gist of the behavior. An example for a fictitious and slightly odd company highly concerned with employee nutrition could be *Eating and Drinking*. The title is followed by a definition that embellishes what is meant by the title. So our definition could read *"Consume enough food and drink during the day to ensure that they are happy and healthy to take on work challenges."*

Close on the heels of the definition are the specific observable traits that ensure a competency is robust and defensible. Common practice dictates that competencies should be defined by a set of behavioral indicators, which is jargon for a series of short statements that would describe whether a person is satisfying the competency. These indicators should be discrete (only represented once in the framework), observable in the workplace, and measurable (where a positive or negative score could be given). Back to our competency of *Eating and Drinking,* I might provide the behavioral indicators of *"Eats lunch at 1 p.m. each workday, but not at his or her desk; consumes a healthy balance of types of food, inclusive of two servings of vegetables or fruits a day; uses the microwave only for food that will not irritate co-workers (i.e., no leftovers)."*

For any given role, it is recommended that six to eight behavioral competencies be selected, each with the same structure of title, definition, and behavioral indicators. This recommendation is thought to balance the need to cover the variety of work inherent to any job with the need to focus on the competencies most related to overall job performance. Identifying over eight competencies can result in an unwieldy assessment regime that does not adequately identify the right types of job candidates.

Complementing behavioral competencies are the skills, knowledge, and experiences that enable performance, often referred to as technical competencies or capabilities. Personally, I like to use the word *capability* here to minimize confusion with behavioral competencies. A technical capability framework takes account of all the certifications, education, and on-the-job learning that individuals acquire in their careers.

Capabilities answer a different question. An employee can possess all the training required to do a job (has the technical capability), but not apply this learning to the job (lacks competency performance). The process of defining capabilities is similar, with job analysis used to identify a focused list of qualifications, certifications, or training attained by employees, as well as experience working in a given job, geography, or industry. A definition is drafted and some examples provided about what demonstrate the fulfillment of the capability. Yet, unlike a competency that can be evaluated across a range of effectiveness (a scale running from very effective to not effective at all), a technical capability is binary (an employee either has attained a qualification or has not).

To illustrate what a technical capability could look like, our fictitious employer who is overly concerned with employee nutrition could define the capability of *Lunch Safety* as "*Attended a half-day, in-company course on the five food groups, using cutlery, and storing leftovers, which will not be consumed on company grounds.*" The capability could also include alternative ways of demonstrating fulfillment, for example, through the completion of "*A food nutrition or personal training certification.*"

There is a temptation to create a laundry list of capabilities that an individual should have and, taken to the extreme, there will be very few candidates or employees who will meet these requirements. Eight competencies and eight capabilities provides plenty of scope to make a decision, even without considering an individual's job performance or motivational profile. Focus is key, and we as practitioners are responsible for deciding which competencies and capabilities to include in the final mix.

Now we come to the complex part. Coming up with behavioral competencies and technical capabilities is a fairly straightforward task if considering a single job. You perform some job analysis with a representative group of job incumbents and managers, this information is then synthesized into competency and capability definitions that are circulated around to your experts for approval. They make some changes. Job done.

Yet, what happens when you are tasked with creating an organization-wide competency or capability framework that can represent hundreds of jobs and thousands of employees? There are not enough days to allow for a full job analysis, let alone the writing and validation of the resulting frameworks. The task of building organization-wide frameworks is thus littered with tradeoffs. I demonstrate below the choices practitioners make to create practical and scalable frameworks.

## The Tradeoffs

In my opinion, there is only one universal truth when it comes to building a competency or capability framework. This truth asserts that *a perfect framework does not exist, but rather all frameworks will fail to a greater or lesser extent.*

This is a bold statement that contradicts an industry built around talent management. There is no shortage of consultants who tout their ability to build a framework that will drive business success for their clients. Other consultants go further by claiming that they have already solved this problem by identifying a list of characteristics that are universal to successful employees across industries and geographies.

This just doesn't feel right, as compromises are unavoidable whenever a practitioner builds a framework. Any abstraction beyond a single employee working in a specific job and the competency and capability requirements begin losing their credibility. Aggregating roles, geographies, functions, or levels collectively results in a framework's failure to adequately address the variance in how staff perform their jobs and the skills that they need along the way.

I was once told an anecdote about how Napoleon chose the uniforms for his army. In order to save money and time, he decided to tailor all uniforms based upon the measurements of the average soldier and, of course, the resulting uniforms were a disaster. The sleeves were too short for some, the waist too loose for others, and only a few soldiers felt comfortable in their new duds. True or not, the same applies here. Taking broad generalizations about jobs and workgroups loses precious detail.

So the real question is how close a practitioner can come to identifying the characteristics that have the greatest power to drive performance and engagement on the job, without creating a cumbersome mess of a framework. Ultimately, we want to determine whether frameworks can achieve this tipping point and capture enough information to make informed people decisions. If not, we may need a new approach.

Practitioners make four major tradeoffs when drafting a talent management framework. These choices fall on the same continuum, with greater job detail resulting in a more cumbersome application to hiring, promotion, or development decisions. Practitioners often succumb to the temptation to choose frameworks that are easy to apply, but often fail to recognize key differences between roles.

### CUSTOM OR GENERIC CONTENT

The first decision is whether to create content from scratch or to adopt an existing framework. Creating an organization-specific framework often leads to greater acceptance by employees, as they can see their own history and culture being reflected in its wording. For example, a competency that focuses on customer service is strengthened if it talks about the specific customers and services offered. Sophisticated organizations also see these frameworks as a source of competitive advantage by aligning employees to the behaviors and skills they believe make the biggest difference.

There are situations when an off-the-shelf version may be more appropriate. Many of the frameworks created by human capital consultancies, such as Lominger, have gone through extensive validation, ensuring that competencies are distinct, measurable, and well-written. Similarly, many professional organizations have defined the training and experience seen as essential for people within an industry, which can become the basis of a capability framework. If the organization does not have the appetite or ambition to create a custom framework, adopting a generic alternative may be a valid strategy. Also, if the business environment is likely to change drastically in the short term, this may buy some much-needed time. In practice, many organizations begin by drafting their own frameworks and then use a generic alternative as a reference point.

### LEVELED OR FLAT STRUCTURE

Although organizations are hierarchical by nature, many practitioners choose not to make distinctions in the types of competencies or capabilities they define for their workers. This may seem odd, as the responsibilities held by senior staff are surely different from what would be expected of direct reports. Yet, if the organization is attempting to focus on what is held in common among all workers, in order to embed a behavioral code that employees should adhere to or establish the same base of technical knowledge, a flat structure may be appropriate.

Leveled structures are cumbersome to create, as changes in behavior likely do not escalate the same way that job titles do. For example, on a competency like "following procedures," there may be little to no distinction in what employees at different levels are expected to do. Either they stick to company policy or they don't. Another pitfall for practitioners is to assume that all competencies escalate with greater seniority. In many organizations, proficiency in writing or analysis is highest at the individual contributor level, which calls into question whether these competencies should hit a plateau or even be adjusted downward for senior staff.

### FUNCTIONAL OR ORGANIZATIONAL SPAN

A similar decision is made about whether a framework is broken up by function, with distinct content that applies only to be given function, or tailored for organization-wide competencies or capabilities. Functional frameworks link more directly to what employees are asked to do in their jobs and, therefore, are generally more accepted when used for people decisions. Moreover, functional leaders feel empowered when asked to build a framework and are often only too happy to speak about what makes their divisions unique.

On the other hand, functional structures jar with efforts to create a common code of behavior across an organization. A greater number of functional models can muddy the waters about what is valued, in addition to increasing the responsibility for practitioners to keep the frameworks current. If employees are performing similar jobs, but happen to fall into different divisions, the standard that they are held accountable for may differ between functions, leading to inconsistencies in promotion and rewards. In practice, a middle state is possible and often employed by my clients, whereby certain competencies and capabilities are identified to cut across the organization, balanced by core differences spelled out by functional leaders.

### SEPARATE OR BLENDED CONTENT

I have purposely made distinctions between the content underlying job analysis, for example, in the labeling of my five key ingredients or in defining competencies as distinct from capabilities. When it comes to framework design, a great many clients I have worked with have

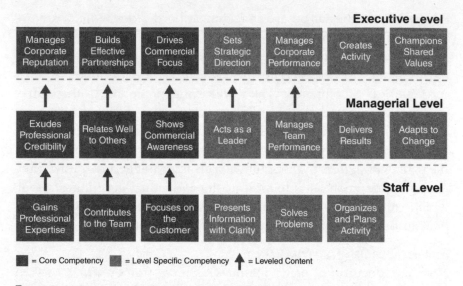

■ = Core Competency  ■ = Level Specific Competency  ↑ = Leveled Content

**FIGURE 1.4** Example of a Blended Competency Framework

chosen to blend content in their frameworks, mixing behaviors, skills, and values under a common heading, much to my chagrin. I personally favor keeping competencies separate from capabilities, as they answer different questions. Competencies drive at how individuals go about their jobs, while capabilities highlight the skills, knowledge, and experience that employees should possess. As will be discussed in later chapters, keeping competencies separate from capabilities allows for better assessment and development techniques.

Values are a different story. I find it difficult to understand why an organization would decide to create a separate framework to talk about corporate values. Surely, what an organization values can be expressed in the behaviors expected from its employees. In fact, using value-laden language can bolster the language used in competency definitions, establishing why it is important that employees adopt a similar behavioral code. The example shown (Figure 1.4) is an illustration of how common values can be embedded into a competency framework. The first three competencies in each level represent the cultural pillars the company is founded on.

When building the framework, I made conscious choices about each of the four tradeoffs, which I hoped would best meet the needs of my client. The company wished to create custom content as a means of gaining managerial buy-in and identifying the distinct industry in which it operated. The framework supports three levels of employees (although more actually existed) with both level-specific content and slight changes in competency wording. Functional distinctions were not made, as employees across divisions held similar backgrounds and job titles. Last, three organization-wide values were identified to drive home what everyone in the company held in common.

Although the framework successfully fulfilled my client's requirements, it, too, suffers from the limitations inherent to any framework. By aggregating content into broad competency buckets, detail about an individual job is lost. For a given role in the organization, the wording of the competency can vary in how much it applies to the actual work undertaken by an employee. Moreover, the competencies themselves may vary in how important they are for the employee to perform effectively. These issues are not too different from the fatal flaws talked about for job descriptions (that is, they can be unfocused and vague). The third flaw applies, too, as frameworks are not immune from aging and can become outdated with changes in market conditions, processes, and technology.

As long as the framework is used to guide decisions at the macro level, informing how employees should be interacting across the organization or which skills should be trained universally, they provide a good basis for people decisions. Yet, too often, a framework is relied upon without considering role-specific requirements to make people decisions, informing both reward or selection decisions. More shocking, organizations tend to place an inordinate amount of weight on competencies, especially for post-hire decisions. If you disagree, I would challenge you to think about how much you know about the skills, experience, and motivations of your top-performing staff and co-workers. If you are like most managers I know, you can easily identify behaviors that lead to success, but will struggle to identify commonalities in their backgrounds, training, and work preferences.

## The Good and Bad of Frameworks

In this last section, we will look at how talent management frameworks are used to guide people decisions, specifically, how frameworks are applied to decisions about compensation and to define career paths, topics that are not talked about elsewhere in this book. As you will read later, competency and capability frameworks play a role in virtually all talent management activities.

Beyond deciding what a job is supposed to accomplish, employee compensation is the other fundamental component of any employment relationship. To find an equitable pay level, employers must establish how the job compares to other roles in the organization, as well as how it stacks up against similar jobs available in the broader labor market. Multiple pieces of data come together to establish a compensation band that can be negotiated within, depending on the specific skills and experience of a given job candidate. The bands are generally broad enough to allow for both new recruits and tenured staff to exist in the same range, with some overlap with higher and lower bands. The key is to provide practitioners flexibility in their pay negotiations.

Evaluation is the process of comparing jobs based on the organization's determinants of worth. Worth can be based on a number of different yardsticks, for example, revenue brought into the organization, innovation of products or services, smart investments, or customer service. In order for a specific yardstick to be considered valid and fair, it has to fulfill the following criteria:

- Be present in all jobs being evaluated (that is, consistently applied to a job family).
- Vary in degree between jobs (for example, senior sales jobs have higher revenue targets).
- Are unambiguous, distinct, and observable in the work employees accomplish.
- Convey meaning to both the employee and organization (that is, not arbitrary).

When evaluating jobs, practitioners vary their approach, depending on how far they want to go down the rabbit hole. If the job is not core to the business, they might favor grouping jobs across their organization into a basic hierarchy of pay levels, based on level of responsibility (for example, whether they manage teams or not). More sophisticated practitioners will classify jobs into meaningful groups (function, region, etc.) and evaluate each job within that group, with an eye toward maintaining parity between groups. The most in-depth approach is to conduct a factor-by-factor comparison of all jobs, coming up with a mechanism to compensate jobs by their unique combination of factors. With any of these approaches, practitioners utilize labor market data (salary surveys, job postings, purchasing power between locations, etc.) as a reference point, to ensure that they are making informed choices about how they are compensating their employees and whether they want to be seen as good employers.

The best-known model for evaluation is offered by Hay, where universal factors place jobs into 15 percent pay intervals that are then tailored to each organization. The Hay model takes account of four primary factors. First, how much know-how is expected of the job incumbent in terms of procedures and techniques, breadth of management skills, and interpersonal skills. Second, how much the employee engages in active problem solving when reacting to the business environment, as well as the challenges he or she faces. Third, how much accountability the employee holds, his or her freedom to act, and likely impact on business results. The fourth factor involves extreme working conditions and only applies to a fraction of jobs, like those poor folks who clean out our sewers. When you look at the Hay system, it is plain to see the competencies and capabilities that underlie it. The application of these criteria to specific organizations and jobs allows for equitable compensation decisions.

As a second application for talent management frameworks, career paths draw out the relationships between jobs in an organization for employees to understand and plan their career trajectories. In an excellent book written by one of my colleagues, Gary Carter details the content underlying a career path as including qualifications (education, training, and certificates), critical developmental experiences, behavioral and technical competencies, and career success factors, which are all very similar to the five key ingredients that I personally focus on when conducting a job analysis.

Just like any other job analysis, pulling together a career path involves interviews with job incumbents and managers, observations of work performed, and surveys. Yet, unlike other analyses, information about the strength of a relationship between two jobs is sometimes included (expressed as a percentage of hires coming from the previous role), as well as information about average salary, typical seniority in role, and industry trends and outlook.

By laying out how the characteristics of jobs change, it becomes obvious to employees what they need to demonstrate to move up within the organization or take a lateral job assignment. I've seen some excellent career portals that show these relationships visually, providing employees a query function to see what is different between their own jobs and others in the company. It is only a matter of time before these systems become even more sophisticated, allowing employees to audit their own personal backgrounds (rather than relying on job title) to see how they might fit other parts of the business.

The benefits are not limited to employees. If the organization wants to redeploy staff, identify skills gaps, or tap a different talent pool, career path information can be invaluable. For example, I was recently given an opportunity to define the career paths for a large national retail bank. What shocked me most about this project was the central importance of the financial planner role. If an employee worked in this position, gaining the associated skills and experience, he or she could literally move across the bank, taking jobs in head office, retail banking, or business and private banking. Until the career path was defined, my client had not realized the crucial importance of the role and the answers it provided for workforce planning. Investing in this role was key to providing a steady stream of qualified bankers.

From these two examples, you are probably wondering what's wrong with the use of talent management frameworks? In premise, nothing. Using frameworks provides the criteria by which really important talent management decisions are made and, without them, the chance of abuse goes up immensely. Where I find fault with current practice is in the content of the frameworks, as well as organizational leaders unknowingly using inappropriate frameworks to guide their decisions.

Earlier in this chapter, I argued that job descriptions and frameworks are often unfocused, vague, and outdated. I have personally seen a number of global and powerful companies adopt a list of ten or so behavioral competencies, undifferentiated by function or level and not updated to account for organizational changes, for use in major decisions involving reward and promotion. Not only can this be dangerous ground if anyone challenged the decisions, but from a practical perspective, I find it hard to believe that these behaviors are driving performance equally across the organization. Why would I assume that the same behaviors apply to both customer-facing and admin roles, or alternatively front-line staff and corporate executives?

I'm not the first to raise such concerns, and others take a hard line with the general failures of job analysis. For example, Dr. Singh from York University in Toronto argues that traditional job analysis is inherently flawed, due to its assumptions that jobs are static, incumbents share the same way to approach a job, and that key activities lie with the individual (rather than shared by a team).

Lazy job analysis leads to irrelevant job descriptions and frameworks that defeat the purpose of having solid criteria to make important talent management decisions against. Unfortunately, I find comprehensive frameworks the exception rather than the rule. Even when strong methods are used in evaluating jobs for compensation and reward, seldom do these models make their way to recruiters and development teams. It is almost like the organization has amnesia about how compensation bands were created. Instead, the larger organization is stuck using frameworks with a bias toward behaviors, ignoring functional and level differences, and is often maladjusted to current organizational pressures.

Practitioners have the opportunity to set the story straight by refocusing leaders on the jobs, activities, and worker characteristics that matter most to current and future performance. By making the criteria for people decisions more focused, specific, and current, leaders will be able to spot talent more effectively, deploy them in the right places, and make investments to grow organizational capability even further. This is not a simple task, and it requires a great deal of influence and confidence on the part of the practitioner. The easier option will always be to adopt frameworks that are quick and cheap to implement.

Like the other topics discussed in this book, you have to make the call about whether you are satisfied with the criteria used in your organization and, if not, whether the battle is worth fighting. There are many more practices to explore in the following chapters, each with the potential to improve the employment relationship.

# Chapter 2

## Talent Acquisition

As any recent graduate can attest, trying to find a job is a horrendous process. The time invested in researching potential employers, filling out applications, undergoing assessment, and deciding what to do once you receive a job offer, is immense. For those already employed, the process can create inertia against changing employers. On one hand, they might not be happy in their current jobs, but on the other, they don't want to invest the time and energy to embark on a full-fledged job search. In weighing the pros and cons of either sticking with the devil they know or putting themselves out into the job market, many talented individuals make the decision to stay put.

Reflecting back on my first job, the world has changed considerably for job-seekers. I remember driving around to all the local shops and gathering application forms from retailers, selected by whether I was interested in their employee discount. Putting on what I considered my best clothes, I would return the applications and hope for an interview on the spot, which is actually how I landed my first job. Later, I worked in a government office helping young people find jobs in the local community. Working from a rudimentary system, we were able to input and then print out job postings. By the time we received the job order, input the information, and dispersed it to the branch offices, it was often too late, with the job filled by candidates walking through the door.

Fast forwarding to today's labor market, résumés can be submitted with a click of a button. Job boards provide countless opportunities, but in some ways have created more work for the applicant. The process has changed from finding opportunities to sifting through information. Knowing what to look for, focusing on jobs that have the greatest potential fit, and then tailoring the response (application, résumé, and cover letter) are skills that have taken on greater importance for the modern job-seeker. With many employers using key word searches and very specific screening questions to find only the most qualified candidates, applicants need to adjust their responses to demonstrate how they specifically fit a job opening.

The role of technology has likewise dramatically increased the workload of recruiters. Bersin and Associates (2011) report that the average company receives 144 applications per every entry-level opening and eighty-nine applications for every professional job. Well-known brands and highly sought after jobs may receive an even greater number of applications, breaching into the range of 1,000 applications per job. Like candidates, the world of recruitment has changed from creating visibility for job opportunities to weeding through a mess of résumés to find the right talent.

It is no wonder that internal candidates, employee referrals, and professional networks still play heavily in successful hires. Bersin and Associates found that 45 percent of jobs were filled in this way, where applicants are known to the organization. That still leaves a considerable number of positions being filled with applicants outside of the immediate network. They report that 19 percent of candidates are placed via job boards, 13 percent through the company website, 9 percent via agencies, 7 percent from universities, and 3 percent resulting from print and newspapers. The remaining 4 percent reflects a combination of social networking and other channels.

In this chapter, we will look at how companies go about attracting talent, taking a deep dive into the burgeoning field of *employer branding*. We'll see that the process of finding talent requires a great deal of effort for candidates and employers alike. The key to a successful talent acquisition strategy is not to increase the volume of applications, but rather to increase the quality of candidates. Making a company appealing is not the same thing as targeting applicants with the greatest chances of landing the job and then having a fruitful career with the company. Transparency and trust play a large part in a talent acquisition strategy, allowing for candidates and recruiters to evaluate the level of fit between them. I will demonstrate that employer branding is an area that deserves investment, as there is no way to unwind the technology that now drives the recruitment process.

## More Than a Single Brand

Every year, business news outlets (fed by consultancies) put out their lists of the top companies to work for. Not only are these lists a great read for graduates hitting the job market, but they are a way for companies to escape criticism and obtain some positive attention. The fads that go along with these lists are numerous, from flexible benefits schemes, where employees can trade between time off, club memberships, or even merchandise, to working practices like Google's "20 percent time," where staff were given one day a week to experiment on side projects.

Although Google reshaped this perk last year, they still feature at the top of the 2014 list of *Fortune* magazine's 100 Best Companies to Work For. Fueled by the Great Place to Work Institute, the survey has captured responses from approximately 6,000 organizations, from fifty countries, representing more than ten million employees. The yardstick used to define the top companies is centered on trust: whether employees can trust the people they work for, have pride in what they do, and enjoy the people they work with. Employee trust is said to be created through management *credibility*, the *respect* they experience, and the extent to which they believe they are treated with *fairness*.

Companies go about creating a great place to work by demonstrating excellence in nine practice areas, categorized into the way organizational goals are pursued, whether employees are encouraged to try their best, and whether employees work as a team. By keeping the model consistent across years and inviting the same list of companies to take part in the survey, the Great Place to Work Institute is able to provide a perspective as to which companies are treating their employees well and the trends among them. Over the course of my career, I have witnessed companies taking these rankings very seriously, setting an executive board–level target to appear in the top 100 companies.

These organizations are convinced that making the list will have significant financial benefits. Beyond the kudos and positive marketing of being featured in *Fortune*, the Great Place to Work Institute boasts that companies in the top 100 outperform their peers (with a comparative annualized stock market return of 11.80 percent against the S&P 500 average of 6.04 percent between 1997 and 2013), as well as have significantly lower turnover against industry norms.

I have often wondered whether this relationship is a chicken and egg problem. Does a high level of trust between employers and their staff create successful environments, or is it the opposite? Successful companies generally have the capital to invest in employees, the freedom to take time in decision making, and the appeal to hire and retain the best talent. It would be hard to imagine that organizations undergoing significant change (whether created from within or thrust upon them by external forces) could successfully retain the high level of trust measured in the survey. Change often forces decisions to be made quickly without the full consultation of employees, as well as the potential to turn the whole employment relationship on its head.

My guess is that the relationship is more like a virtuous cycle, where success breeds further success. Nonetheless, a list of the top twenty-five companies for 2014 includes the following companies:

1. Google
2. SAS
3. The Boston Consulting Group
4. Edward Jones
5. Quicken Loans
6. Genentech
7. Salesforce.com
8. Intuit
9. Robert W. Baird and Co.
10. DPR Construction
11. Camden Property Trust
12. Wegmans Food Markets
13. David Weekley Homes
14. Burns and McDonnell
15. Hilcorp
16. CHG Healthcare Services
17. USAA

**18.** Southern Ohio Medical Center
**19.** Baptist Health
**20.** Ultimate Software
**21.** Kimpton Hotels and Restaurants
**22.** W.L. Gore and Associates
**23.** Plante Moran
**24.** Scripps Health
**25.** Atlantic Health System

Glassdoor adopts a totally different approach in establishing their list of top companies. Instead of actively measuring companies against an established model, they rely on job incumbents to provide anonymous feedback about their employers. The list of top companies is based purely on the data captured in a given year about each employee's level of satisfaction with both the job and the company, as well as feelings about career opportunities, compensation and benefits, work-life balance, and senior leadership. Their list of the top twenty-five companies for 2014 looks like this:

**1.** Bain and Company
**2.** Twitter
**3.** LinkedIn
**4.** Eastman Chemical
**5.** Facebook
**6.** Guidewire
**7.** Interactive Intelligence
**8.** Google
**9.** Orbitz Worldwide
**10.** Nestle Purina PetCare
**11.** John Deere
**12.** Edelman
**13.** Qualcomm
**14.** Chevron
**15.** Slalom Consulting
**16.** Costco Wholesale
**17.** Riverbed Technology
**18.** SolarCity
**19.** Intuit

**20.** Gartner
**21.** Southwest Airlines
**22.** MathWorks
**23.** Red Hat
**24.** Cameron
**25.** Genentech

A limitation of the above list might rest in the sampling of employees. Not every employee will go onto the website and write a review of his or her employer. We can assume that employees will only be motivated to do so when they have something to say, either positive or negative. Other employers might avoid taking part, in fear that their posts will not be truly anonymous. That said, this approach is a grassroots approach to what the Great Place to Work Institute does through their methodology.

A completely different list of top companies is provided by Universum and featured in *BusinessWeek*, which, instead of relying on job incumbents for their opinions, look to job hunters. The 2014 survey was completed by 46,000 undergraduate students in the United States who were asked to rate their "ideal" employer. The results for this list include the following:

**1.** Google
**2.** Walt Disney Company
**3.** Apple
**4.** Ernst and Young
**5.** J.P. Morgan
**6.** Deloitte
**7.** PwC
**8.** Nike
**9.** Goldman Sachs
**10.** KPMG
**11.** Amazon
**12.** Microsoft
**13.** Major League Baseball
**14.** The Coca-Cola Co.
**15.** FBI
**16.** Morgan Stanley

17. NBCUniversal
18. Nordstrom
19. Procter & Gamble
20. U.S. Department of State
21. Bank of America Merrill Lynch
22. Target
23. Facebook
24. U.S. Department of the Treasury
25. Starbucks

When these lists are put side by side, a few trends become apparent. Only one company appears in the top twenty-five on every list, Google. Beyond this, Genentech and Intuit appear twice (reported by both the Great Place to Work Institute and Glassdoor as good companies to work for), while Facebook appears on Glassdoor's and Universum's lists of ideal employers. Clearly, these lists are measuring different things.

Another and less obvious trend is the type of companies that are appearing in the top twenty-five (Figure 2.1). Technology companies are apparent across all three lists, yet other industries are disproportionately represented in a single list. For example, healthcare companies pop up on the Great Place to Work list, whereas accountancy firms and government agencies appear only on Universum's ideal employer list.

If you are wondering which list you should trust, I would argue that all three are interesting and meaningful in their own way. This exercise is a great way to introduce the ways in which marketing and talent acquisition interact. For example, the power of a company's corporate brand is most evident in the Universum list of ideal employers. This survey captures the brand recognition of potential employees. Some involved graduates may actually be aware of what these big name organizations offer their staff in terms of employment, but my guess is that the majority have an affinity for the consumer brand and want to be part of it.

The other two lists are getting closer to the reality of the employment relationship, albeit in terms defined by the creators of the list. With each organization trying to define itself in a way that is uniquely meaningful to its current and potential employees, comparison

| | Great Place to Work | Glassdoor | Universum |
|---|---|---|---|
| 1 | Google | Bain and Company | Google |
| 2 | SAS | Twitter | Walt Disney Company |
| 3 | The Boston Consulting Group | LinkedIn | Apple |
| 4 | Edward Jones | Eastman Chemical | Ernst and Young |
| 5 | Quicken Loans | Facebook | J.P. Morgan |
| 6 | Genentech | Guidewire | Deloitte |
| 7 | Salesforce.com | Interactive Intelligence | PwC |
| 8 | Intuit | Google | Nike |
| 9 | Robert W. Baird and Co. | Orbitz Worldwide | Goldman Sachs |
| 10 | DPR Construction | Nestle Purina PetCare | KPMG |
| 11 | Camden Property Trust | John Deere | Amazon |
| 12 | Wegmans Food Markets | Edelman | Microsoft |
| 13 | David Weekley Homes | Qualcomm | Major League Basebal |
| 14 | Burns and McDonnell | Chevron | The Coco-Cola Co. |
| 15 | Hilcorp | Slalom Consulting | FBI |
| 16 | CHG Healthcare Services | Costco Wholesale | Morgan Stanley |
| 17 | USAA | Riverbed Technology | NBCUniversal |
| 18 | Southern Ohio Medical Center | SolarCity | Nordstrom |
| 19 | Baptist Health | Intuit | Procter and Gamble |
| 20 | Ultimate Software | Gartner | US Department of State |
| 21 | Kimpton Hotels and Restaurants | Southwest Airlines | Bank of America Merrill Lynch |
| 22 | W.L. Gore and Associates | MathWorks | Target |
| 23 | Plante Moran | Red Hat | Facebook |
| 24 | Scripps Health | Cameron | US Department of the Treasury |
| 25 | Atlantic Health System | Genentech | Starbucks |

FIGURE 2.1   Three Lists of the Top Twenty-Five Companies

would not be possible unless some sort of common yardstick were used. In the case of the Great Place to Work Institute, trust and its derivatives are used as the benchmark. For Glassdoor, it is a combination of career opportunities, compensation and benefits, work-life balance, and quality of senior leadership.

In the sections below, we will dig more deeply into how organizations work to attract and retain talent. I demonstrate that it is an effortful process to understand what is unique and meaningful about a specific employer and then translate this into a message that targets the right type of talent. Although good at grabbing the headlines, top employer lists do not do justice to the type of work undertaken in employer branding. Moreover, when the employer brand is ill-conceived, not matching reality, or poorly managed, the whole corporate reputation is on the line. In a socially connected world, it only takes a few seconds for a bad experience to do its damage.

## Let's Be Realistic

As a starting place for creating or refreshing a talent acquisition strategy, practitioners need to know what is on offer in their specific place of employment. They need to know what it is that makes their organization like no other, both positively and negatively. Only then will they have a platform to build the talent acquisition strategy around.

The term *employer value proposition* (EVP) is used by practitioners to describe the workplace reality. Towers Watson (2012) defined EVP as "the collective array of programs that an organization offers in exchange for employment. It is also referred to as the employment deal." The Society for Human Resource Management (SHRM) provides a similar definition in 2008, stating that EVP involves the culture, systems, attitudes, and nature of employee relationships within an organization. Glassdoor in 2014 provides a more condensed definition, referring to EVP as "the complete package of reasons for jobseekers to choose to work for your company."

The characteristics that encompass the EVP extend from the tangible, such as the level of compensation and the number of work hours, to the intangible, such as the values that employees aspire toward. Hill and Tande (2006) speak about how the emphasis is often placed on the tangible, especially on compensation and benefits, when thinking about the drivers of employee recruitment and retention. The temptation lies in its visible and quantifiable nature. Like the features of the top companies to work for, it provides ready comparison between very different companies.

Yet, compensation sits much lower down the list of why employees leave their places of employment, beaten out by features like limited advancement, unhappiness with management, and lack of recognition. These are softer features of the employment relationship that beg for further exploration. For example, exactly what was it about the manager that made the employee leave? Was the manager a micro-manager, poorly skilled, or unethical? The answer to this question points to a different type of workplace feature; a commonality in expectation about the role of management and how they are to interact with employees. Because there is no one single way to effectively work with others, comparisons between companies on these types of workplace features requires a different approach. We'll come back to this point shortly.

To stir thinking and help companies to look beyond the tangible, Hill and Tande ask: "What would we say or do to attract and retain people if we had to pay 20 percent below market?" In future chapters, we will look at the issue of motivation in more detail, but this line of thinking is very similar to the distinction between hygiene factors (workplace characteristics that require basic fulfillment) and true motivators that engage and drive maximum performance (such as finding true interest in the subject matter).

Without thinking about it or doing anything, every company has an EVP of sorts. Each company has an established way of working, with behavioral norms, systems, and processes in place that shape how employees work together. But this is not the point. Smart organizations look at this reality, think about the implications of their EVP for attracting and retaining talent, and then do something about it.

Surveys of existing employees are a common way to start gaining a perspective on EVP. Job incumbents are asked a series of questions about what they desire from their employers, as well as their current experience along these same dimensions. Although a survey is not necessarily open-ended, it can provide a thorough audit of workplace characteristics. Survey topics include features such as compensation and benefits, what employees are tasked to do, impressions of their immediate team, opportunities to develop and grow, and characteristics about the organization itself (for example, whether it is a household name and adheres to a set of guiding principles).

Each one of these domains is broken down further, to gain a clearer reading on what truly matters to employees. For example, compensation may be broken down into dimensions like financial rewards, health benefits, retirement benefits, stock purchase plans, flexibility of programs, and vacation time.

Such a quantitative approach is a good place to begin, but is not the end all for defining an EVP. As already pointed out, a survey, by design, is limited to the questions asked. The more items asked, the greater the time commitment of participants and the lower the response rate. Therefore, thoroughness of the survey is often compromised (for a good reason) and could miss an essential feature of the workplace, skipped over because the survey designer did not recognize its importance at the start.

For this reason, practitioners will often conduct a series of focus groups and interviews to understand not only what the employee experience is like, but what it will likely be in the future. Towers Watson recommends that a diverse range of participants be consulted to build out a fuller picture of the EVP, accounting for age, tenure, geography, and organizational unit. Glassdoor points out that context matters, too, from recently hired employees to attendees at town hall meetings and staff who have decided to leave. Like any other research sample, there is no hard number about who or how many individuals should take part. It should be a carefully constructed representation, with the goal of adding to the quantitative information gained through survey techniques.

From my perspective, the main reason to employ both quantitative and qualitative methods is to ensure that the definition of the EVP does not take on too much of a transactional tone. Tangible aspects of the employment relationship like pay and vacation time are important, but there are other elements to the EVP that are not easy to quantify or compare across organizations. For example, a variety of companies can claim to be driven by an ethical mission, yet driving for environmental sustainability versus driving for consumer value feel very different and, therefore, would attract different types of potential employees. A similar discussion is found later in this book about the two sides of the psychological contract, specifically the relational and transactional. Like talent acquisition, understanding what employees and their workplace hold in common can help drive satisfaction and engagement.

So what does a good EVP look like? To help answer this question, I have solicited feedback from four employer branding experts.

They have helped shape the advice shared in this chapter, from deciding on an EVP to creating an employer brand and activating it in talent acquisition and retention.

Shannon Smedstad is currently the director of employer branding at CEB, having previously set in motion the employer branding strategy at GEICO that was ranked number two for its use of social media in talent communications. Shannon writes for Blogging4Jobs, is a Glassdoor Talent Warrior, and speaks regularly on talent acquisition at professional conferences.

Shannon thinks about EVP as a promise to employees and therefore, she believes that there is an imperative on managers to deliver. She explains that tangible aspects of the workplace (such as pay, benefits, and working hours) are rolled up into an overarching promise about how employees are to be treated. Employees hold their manager and the organization accountable for delivering on the promises that they have set.

Asking current employees about their experience provides an indication of whether expectations are being fulfilled; however, she cautions against relying solely on online information sources. Employees are known to "write when they have something to say," with a tendency for comments to focus on the negative. She explains that a more holistic approach would involve researching the perceptions of new hires, employees who are exiting the business, candidates who turned down offers of employment, general staff opinion surveys, and targeted interviews with executives. The practitioner's job is then to find the "common positive threads," which can be communicated with candidates in a balanced, authentic, and transparent way.

Finding über themes in the data from multiple stakeholders is also a goal for Rob O'Keefe, vice president at TMP Worldwide Advertising and Communications. With thirty years of advertising and marketing experiences working alongside some of the best-respected companies in their industries, Rob has seen the evolution of employer branding from a concept to a practice that no company should do without. A featured speaker at HR conferences and frequent author on employer brand development, Rob brings a practitioner's view on how to effectively embark on a branding exercise.

Rob stresses that, when designing research to uncover an organization's EVP, not all constituencies should necessarily have equal weight. Similar to the process of thinking through which consumer groups are a priority, there exists a hierarchy of talent pools when developing an EVP. Priorities can be set by the company's needs for placing and retaining critical, high volume, or historically hard-to-fill positions. Practitioners also need to decide whether they should consult a wide array of employees or focus solely on the most engaged and highest potential employees. Determining the balance of voices in the EVP conversation allows for both an overarching view of the employment experience and clearer patterns about why key talent joined the company and the culture that keeps them there.

Yet, in a world of social media, there is no limit to the number of individuals vying to be heard. As mentioned in the next section, employer brand is about perception and, because of this, completely ignoring the sentiments of any person engaging with the brand would be foolhardy. Rob's point is that it is up to the practitioner to determine how to arrive at an EVP that speaks to everyone, while allowing for opportunities to make the EVP message even more compelling for key groups.

Once the über themes have been identified, the organization has to decide what to do with them. Some organizations decide to popularize their EVP directly, putting it up on a website for current and future employees to see. For example, Deloitte Australia talks about their EVP on their MyCareer website, first generically explaining what an EVP is and then detailing the research process that derived their specific EVP. The resulting fourteen statements are believed to be an authentic and aspirational view about working at the firm. A few of the EVP statements include: "Creativity is encouraged; innovation is expected," "We believe teamwork beats individual brilliance every time," and "We have a playful culture with serious intent."

Although such an approach demonstrates confidence that the firm can deliver on topics like innovation, teamwork, and playfulness, these statements might not really connect with outsiders to the culture. Rob suggests that communicating the EVP can best be accomplished through brand articulation. He believes that the greatest challenge to practitioners is finding a creative and relevant story to tell from EVP themes, which then can be "dialed-up or dialed-down" depending on the target group. How to do this effectively is the topic of the next section.

## Compelling Themes

Unlike a lot of the other practices talked about in this book, the notion of *employer brand* is a relatively new concept. The first formalized manifestation of the term appeared in the *Journal of Brand Management* in 1996, in an article by Tim Ambler and Simon Barrow. They asserted that a marketing approach to talent is viable and that, if a positive employment experience can be expressed in a way similar to a product brand, the benefits could extend beyond recruitment to an improved customer experience.

The late 1990s provided a perfect environment for the topic to gain traction as an essential feature of talent acquisition. With low unemployment, the emergence of technology that began to connect potential applicants with companies, and a rigid belief that there was a war for talent underway, companies flocked to the concept. By 2008, the Society for Human Resource Management (SHRM) found that 61 percent of companies reported having a formalized employer brand, with an additional 25 percent stating that they either recently established it or planned to do so in the next year. Eighty-one percent of the HR professionals polled stated that they had a strategy in place to leverage their employer brand to attract talent, while 69 percent planned to do so with employee retention.

Companies are also investing in their employer brand. CEB reports in 2014 that companies spend on average $193,000 annually on employer branding, which equates to about $3 per application. Of this budget, 24 percent is spent on professional and social media, 17 percent on job board and aggregators, 10 percent on creative, and only 5 percent on branding research and measurement. From my perspective, the potential payoff of a well-constructed employer brand more than pays for itself, and the amount allocated to measurement is shockingly low (equating to only $9,750 annually). A lot can happen to a brand in a year and, without measuring this change, I'm not sure how effective the overall strategy can be.

Now that we know of its importance, how can we define an employer brand? I mentioned earlier that most practitioners see it as an aggregate perception of an employer. SHRM defines an employer brand as the image of the organization "as a great place to work in the minds of current employees and key stakeholders in the external market (active and passive candidates, clients, customers, and other key stakeholders." What is interesting about this definition is its emphasis on people outside of the organization, rather than current employees.

Glassdoor's *Employer Branding for Dummies*, published in 2014, makes more room for both internal and external stakeholders, defining employer brand as a company's *reputation* as a place of employment. Universum differs slightly in its definition, focusing more on the relative position of a company against its peers. Employer brand is defined as the identity of a company as an *employer of choice*.

No matter which of these definitions is utilized, the common thread is that employer brand is about perception. In the words of Shannon Smedstad, it is "perceptions of what everyone else says it is." Employer branding is the process by which companies go about attempting to shape and influence this perception. Universum defines the branding process as the way a company promotes itself as an employer of choice among a desired target group (the group of talent that a company wants to recruit and retain).

Initially, employer branding was about building visibility. Shannon reflected on her first forays into employer branding at GEICO, when their initial goal was to drive the number of applicants to apply for volume jobs. Shannon stated that her company "needed to create mass appeal and let people know that we were hiring." A lot changed in the years that followed, with GEICO becoming much more sophisticated in its approach, landing a variety of accolades for the quality of its employer branding.

Across the sources I consulted in writing this chapter, there were a few recurrent and easily identified features of a strong employer brand. Strong brands are:

- ◆ *Impactful.* The brand needs to resonate well with current and potential employees.
- ◆ *Credible.* It needs to be a fair reflection of what actually exists.
- ◆ *Aspirational.* The brand should go beyond the tangible and address the culture.
- ◆ *Distinctive.* It should set itself apart from other talent competitors.
- ◆ *Consistent.* The brand should not conflict with the corporate strategy or values.

To make the connection between EVP and employer brand, Rob O'Keefe describes the two concepts as the convergence of art and science. The process of identifying an EVP is driven by science and experience; qualitative and quantitative data is captured, analyzed, and used to determine a few differentiating themes.

How this information is transformed into the creative articulation of a brand is about the art of communication. In the artistic process, Rob suggests one think equally about talent acquisition and employee retention, pointing out that "people make the voluntary act of staying at work every day."

From Shannon Smedstad's perspective, branding is about giving trusted guidance to current and future employees to gage whether a company is the right fit. By providing key messages about what a company is like, practitioners can encourage people to act. For talent acquisition, it is about persuading the right type of candidates to apply. For job incumbents, it is about encouraging employees to engage with the brand and act as brand ambassadors.

Shannon reminds practitioners that companies don't own their brands. The best companies can do is influence perception by positioning the company in a certain light in the minds of current and prospective employees. Content drives changes in perception and, therefore, asking compelling questions like "What stories inside the company are worth sharing?" "What is it really like on a typical day?" or "What makes this place truly unique?" can help build the right story.

Just like EVP, the employer brand should be generally consistent across target groups. For example, GEICO had ten entry points into the organization across sixteen locations, resulting in a potential of 160 separate brands. Instead of allowing brands to organically arise across a company, a better approach is to create a consistent brand presence, with the opportunity for slight tailoring to be made, depending on the audience. For example, different imagery or accents can be used to tailor the message across geographies.

As examples of what an employer brand could look like, SHRM included some notable brands in their research from 2008. Each of these employer brands sets an expectation about the employment relationship, as felt on a day-to-day basis by their particular EVP:

- ◆ *Microsoft:* How far can your potential take you?
- ◆ *Johnson & Johnson:* Small-company environment. Big-company impact.

- ◆ **AT&T:** Exciting Positions. Energized Environment. Cutting-Edge Technology.
- ◆ **Charles Schwab:** We're looking for a different kind of employee.
- ◆ **Nike:** We're all about sports. And then some.

Since all the above are household names, a decision had to be made about how close the employer brand stands relative to the consumer brand. Mokina in 2014 positions employer brand as one of four potential brands sitting within the overall corporate brand, the others being the product brand (for business to consumer relationships), social brand (for business to government relationships), and goodwill (for business to business relationships).

Among these four, the product brand has the greatest impact on the employer brand, by reinforcing the power that it has in the minds of current and future employees. With reported correlations in the range of .60 to .80 between employee satisfaction and consumer satisfaction, ignoring the linkage between the two types of brands could be disastrous. Not every company will be able to leverage its product brand, but in the minimum, the two types of brands should not be in conflict with each other.

To help bring this section to life, it is time to introduce the third employer branding expert I interviewed. Lars Schmidt is the founder of AmplifyTalent, having previously worked as senior director at NPR, where he transformed the talent acquisition function from reactionary to one that fully leveraged social media. Before NPR, he was a vice president at Ticketmaster, responsible for recruitment, employee development, and internal communications. A frequent blogger, Lars has been named as one of the top 100 Influencers in Human Resources by *HR Examiner* and in the top 100 Most Social HR Experts on Twitter by the *Huffington Post*.

When Lars took on the challenge of building an employer brand at NPR, the organization was undergoing a time of growth and becoming a multi-media organization. Yet, it had limited recruitment resources (due to its non-profit standing) and faced considerable competition for talent. One thing that NPR had going for it was an incredibly engaged audience that both consumed its products and believed in the organization. In Lars's words, "this definitely gave us an advantage around discovery," at least for some of the talent he was looking for.

For journalists, the consumer brand was appealing and offered a boost to their résumés if they decided to work there. However, this was not the case for IT positions (which were key for the new organizational strategy), as NPR did not yet have a strong reputation for its technology. Moreover, the demographics were different, with many of the younger IT professionals not aware of the NPR brand or consumers of its product.

Lars turned to existing employees who were already tech-savvy to both understand what they enjoyed about working at NPR and to use them as brand ambassadors to attract new talent. By reflecting on NPR's purpose to create a more informed public, he trained his eye to look for talent who were curious, thoughtful, and passionate, no matter whether they were working as journalists or website designers. The employer brand was not owned by one area of the business, but had to extend organization-wide.

"Branding allows HR to become creative," explains Lars. It is about first transitioning prospects into applicants, by building their awareness and engagement with the brand, and then from applicants into candidates, by ensuring that they have the right brand alignment. To build a great brand, Lars advises companies to listen to prospects, applicants, new hires, and job incumbents. By spending more time listening than promoting, a relationship can be built with those involved in the brand, whether they are active applicants, passive prospects, or simply just interested parties.

Attending to the needs of the brand's consumers is something that Susan Strayer LaMotte agrees with. Susan is founder of exaqueo, having previously held the position of senior director of global employer brand and marketing with Marriott. Of her achievements at Marriott, Susan oversaw employer branding for the company's eighteen product brands, managed the company's main careers site, and helped the company attain the top ranking for social recruiting by *Fortune* magazine in 2012. The employer brand itself was awarded Best Employer Brand by ERE. Like Lars, she too is in the top 100 Influencers in Human Resources and in the top 100 Most Social HR Experts.

Susan believes that the employer brand should resonate strongly with current and future employees. Like consumer brands, great care should be taken in attending to the target audience. Practitioners should remind themselves that they "are not selling to everyone" and that being differentiated is a good thing. The employer brand will have a unique set of assets that will resonate differently, depending on who the target is.

She also cautions about being too focused on execution and not taking the time to truly understand the needs of the audience and developing the brand accordingly. Susan puts herself in the mindset of a marketer when developing an employer brand, believing strongly that the same diligence should be taken as if a consumer brand were being established. Employer brands should have a personality, branding elements, and be based on solid pillars that resonate with existing employees, organization leaders, and the external market. Attending to data from employees alone will not ensure success; there has to be a creative element and has to be considered alongside what others are doing in the marketplace. Once developed, testing the brand on new hires or high performers before going live can ensure that the message will land well.

Susan points out that every organization is starting from a different place in developing its employer brand. There are relatively few greenfield opportunities to create an employer brand from scratch. Rather, most organizations have an existing brand (whether or not it is based on a realistic EVP is another issue) that will have to be worked around. Employer branding can be described as a process of adaptation. This is especially true for organizations that have grown through acquisition, where multiple employer brands are in place and practitioners have to balance recruiting for both the parent and acquired companies.

In her time at Marriott, Susan was involved in creating the "Find Your World" employer brand. Although many of the elements of the culture were long-lasting, with employees still describing the company as a family business, Marriott had grown to a new level and was offering greater career opportunities for its employees. What resonated with employees was an action-oriented brand, where they were empowered to find their place in an ever-growing enterprise consisting of eighteen separate consumer brands.

One of the key concepts Susan helped me with is the distinction between an employer brand and a marketing campaign. As with prominent consumer brands, an employer brand should be enduring and talk about something that is core to the business. Making a change, as was done at Marriott, should be done with great caution and with full confidence that the change is necessary. The role of a campaign is to instill vibrancy around the employer brand, taking a new spin on the central message, but not changing its meaning. When looking across the field, I believe that the majority of organizations have not fully appreciated this distinction and go about changing their central employer brand all too often.

## From Message to Market

Coming up with an EVP and an employer brand is an effortful process, but one I think is worth the investment. As a point of comparison, Bersin and Associates in 2011 estimated that the cost for recruiting new talent averages $3,500 per position, with the bulk of the investment spent on job boards and agencies. When a recruiter is used in the hiring process, the cost skyrockets, with the average agency fee equating to 21 percent of the new hire's first year salary. An investment in employer branding (averaging $193,000) can be recouped quickly if these traditional channels can be avoided.

If the branding is done right, better talent will be directed toward the company, which can have an impact beyond lowering the cost of recruitment. SHRM in 2008 reported that employer branding resulted in 55 percent of HR professionals stating that they hired better talent, 49 percent saw stronger qualifications, and 41 percent received more qualified referrals. Regarding internal talent, 24 percent reported greater employee satisfaction, 32 percent saw less turnover, and 11 percent had greater employee productivity. Whenever statistics like these are quoted, it is good to have a healthy dose of skepticism. Companies that are already doing well have the money and aspiration to improve their HR processes. That said, all the indicators point to employer branding being a good thing.

Companies have a multitude of channels that can be exploited to influence perceptions of their brands. Before we delve into what these channels look like and how to create the right balance among them, it is important to note that information sources are not equal in how much people trust them. Glassdoor reported in 2014 that, although 52 percent of potential employees trust friends and family, the level of trust falls dramatically to only 14 percent for company employees, 5 percent for a company website, and 2 percent for a recruiter.

If this research is taken at face value, the best investment a practitioner can make is on the personal network of people already invested in the brand. However, this is not what the average company does. SHRM (2008) reported that the five top actions taken by companies when branding included: 67 percent updating the website, 58 percent highlighting company initiatives, 56 percent developing an organizational tagline, 52 percent communicating the brand, and 47 percent establishing core values. As mentioned below, the experts I consulted are urging companies to take a much more active role in starting a conversation with potential and existing employees to build trust and involvement. Employer branding has moved beyond one-way communication, which might have been prevalent in 2008.

As mentioned earlier, providing transparent and honest depictions of the company is recommended to build trust among potential applicants. One of the easiest ways to move along the continuum from one-way communication to a conversation is to paint a picture of what a day-in-the-life could look like. Displaying pictures of the office, video testimonials from existing employees, and personalized messages from organizational leaders about where the company is going can all help make the content feel more personal and trustworthy.

Better yet, why not allow this content to be organically created? This is the point made by Rob O'Keefe, who argues that the impact of unfiltered (or seemingly unfiltered) information far exceeds what comes out of a centrally controlled process. Employee generated content (EGC) goes further in creating trust and transparency among potential applicants by demonstrating the EVP in the employees' own words and experiences.

Rob suggests that EGC may provide an alternative starting place for understanding the EVP. Such an approach recognizes the growing importance of social media as a primary vehicle for employees to share their experiences, as well as the fact that online content may vary from what arises out of surveys or focus groups. When the EVP is defined through a more traditional research approach and communicated throughout an organization, it can act as a restrictive filter that limits the generation of original and personalized content.

By allowing EGC to arise naturally, practitioners will have organic information to consider when defining the EVP, as well as downstream content that can be shared with the market. The job of the practitioner evolves to that of a content curator and distributor, determining what content to use and balancing brand consistency with content that is more dynamic and relevant. In Rob's words "Employees who take time to create content are engaged. There is something important enough for them to share; why not harness this?"

Lars Schmidt suggests that the opportunity to build better and more relevant content extends throughout the hiring process. For example, Lars finds opportunity in one of the most unexpected places: the job description. Lars states that job descriptions are "one of the least evolved tools in our corporate recruiting tool belt. They are built for compliance, but have potential to create a fuller sense of culture, teams, perks, and the physical office space. We try to convey the soul of the organization in text alone."

Lars envisions a complete makeover of the humble job description, not to undermine the elements required for compliance, but to showcase what the job and company mean to potential employees. For example, why not include short videos from the hiring manager and future colleagues, testimonials from previous employees, and photos of the workspace? All of this could go a long way toward building transparency and trust.

Realistic job previews and more engaging job descriptions are part of a more active approach, but only go so far in having a conversation with potential and existing employees. To build a relationship around the brand, interaction is needed, and this is where social networking plays a part.

Shannon Smedstad shared some staggering facts around social networking. There are 700 YouTube videos shared every minute on Twitter. Every second, two new people join LinkedIn. If Facebook were a country, it would be the third largest in the world. These platforms provide immense opportunity to establish and maintain relationships with people involved in the employer brand. Shannon states that a large number of connections is good, but it is even better when the connections start having conversations around the brand

and what it means to them. She suggests that job incumbents should be encouraged, but not required, to connect with the company's social channels. They should feel empowered to like, share, re-tweet, or comment on posts that they enjoy.

When thinking through what a good piece of content looks like, Shannon suggests that it should be easily consumed by the target audience. The message should be quickly understood and relevant. Text should be succinct and complemented with visuals or audio, with implications for how the content can be supported on mobile technologies. Last, the content should be something that people want to share, to maximize its impact.

Lars Schmidt doesn't disagree that the big three channels for employer branding are Facebook, LinkedIn, and Twitter, although he has a personal fondness for Twitter as the primary tool. At NPR, Lars was able to save over $100,000 in job postings and recruitment marketing by shifting focus to these platforms. All three channels were in the top ten sources of applications and hires by the time he left the organization. Lars believes that the key is to move prospects from discovery to engaging with the brand. Frequent content updates help to move the conversation along. Lars states that you need to give "your followers a reason to keep coming back, engage, and share, regardless of whether they are currently looking for a job." This is especially true among the Millennial generation, who grew up with social media.

To help practitioners deliver on providing timely and relevant content, Lars suggests the use of content aggregators (to find and link the audience to new content), schedulers (to ensure posts go out on a regular basis), and optimization tools (to gage the audience's level of engagement with the content by number of clicks, likes, comments, and shares). Lars emphasizes the need to listen and adapt according to how others are engaging with your content, stating "If you approach status updates as one-way broadcasts, you're missing opportunities to engage more deeply with your community. Your followers clicked because they have an interest in your company, but to really provide value to them, it helps to vary your content to include more than just company updates."

At the far end of the one-way/conversation continuum sit the physical interactions that current and future employees have with people who represent your brand. Shannon Smedstad focuses heavily on the interactions recruiters have with applicants, stating that corporate recruiters might be the only people from the organization a candidate meets. How well do recruiters know the business? How proficient are they in telling the company's story? What lasting impression do they leave? If not doing so already, recruiters and HR staff need to act as "employer brand ambassadors."

Susan Strayer LaMotte also stresses the importance of face-to-face interactions in the overall branding process. She recommends that recruiters be fully trained on the employer brand, from the research that was undertaken to create the brand to how it has been operationalized in the business. Ensuring brand consistency is key, with applicants receiving a similar experience across functions and locations. Practitioners can use techniques like mystery shoppers, a process whereby branding experts go through the hiring process to provide recruiters with feedback. Alternatively, having recruiters describe the company and role in their own words and then comparing it with what their peers heard can highlight differences in messaging.

## How It's Done

As mentioned, attracting and recruiting talent is an effortful process for the potential employee and the hiring organization alike. Although it might be easier today to find a range of opportunities to apply for, the work involved in sifting through job boards and social networking sites, then tailoring your approach to ensure that your skills and experiences are clearly recognized, can be too much to take on. Good talent may find it easier to stick with the employers they know, even if it's not a perfect match, than to embark on a serious job search. The ease of technology has given rise to the passive candidate.

For recruiters, the situation is not much better. Technology has allowed for greater visibility of the employer brand and job opportunities, but it comes at a cost. Specifically, the more popular or attractive the company is as an employer, the greater the risk of poorly qualified candidates flooding the recruitment process. Using key word searches or other screens may help weed out candidates, but I wonder how many good candidates are lost in this process, simply because of a difference in the terminology used. For example, do I call myself an HR practitioner, consultant, talent manager, or all three? Should I highlight work that is not directly relevant for the job or remove it from the application, with the risk that I have intentionally created a sizable gap in my employment history?

It is no wonder that some of the most effective hiring techniques rely on the personal networks of current employees. Internal placements, employee referrals, and close professional networks are the tried-and-true way for candidates and employers to get to know each other, despite risks of a return to an "old boys' club." These channels can stand in opposition to creating a diverse labor pool and may do little to fill positions that are outside the norm. If 55 percent of jobs still require an orientation toward the external labor market, than companies have to become smarter in how they promote themselves and attract only the right types of candidates.

In this chapter, I have outlined what the most thoughtful companies are doing in talent acquisition. By spending the time and energy to know what to offer, create a compelling story around it, and communicate it to the target audience, these organizations are upping the chances that they are recruiting only the most appropriate talent for their particular organizations.

In reality, most organizations are still in the experimental phase of doing talent acquisition well. They have misplaced their talent, simply by not finding it in the first place. When a company approaches the labor market with an unclear or conflicted message, the right type of talent is lost in the shuffle. Job incumbents might question what there is to gain from the employment relationship, let alone whether they should become employer brand ambassadors.

I have identified five key lessons as highlighted by the employer branding experts interviewed for this chapter. I would encourage you to think through how well your own organization (or those that you have worked for in the past) follows these standards:

1. ***Don't focus on quantitative data.*** Employee satisfaction and engagement data, alongside key recruitment KPIs, all play a part in developing an EVP. Use them as indicators about what to explore further through conversation with your stakeholders.

2. ***Maintain consistency in the employer brand.*** Every department and location thinks it is unique. Understand what ties all units together as a collective whole and then dial up or down elements of this message, depending on the target.

3. ***Make the employer brand memorable.*** Just like a consumer brand, it needs to be impactful (mean something to the target), credible (be based on the reality of the workplace), aspirational (be future-focused), distinctive (set itself apart from the competition), and consistent (align well with the corporate strategy).

4. ***Build transparency and trust.*** Not all information is the same when candidates make a decision to join a company. Realistic previews of the job, as well as information coming from trusted sources, allow individuals to make an informed choice about whether the fit is right. The goal is to create a conversation with current and future employees.

5. ***Know the difference between a campaign and brand.*** The employer brand should resonate with what the organization stands for as an employer and, as such, should be relatively stable over time. To rejuvenate hiring, campaigns should be conducted around the brand without displacing it.

I hope that the following case study will bring these messages to life. Of the various companies I work with, I am truly fortunate to partner with the professional, proactive, and incredibly thoughtful talent management group at American Express. In preparing this chapter, I asked Kathleen McCarthy and Christy Mommsen to share the journey American Express has been on in creating a lasting and memorable employer brand.

Kathleen McCarthy is currently senior vice president and chief talent officer for American Express, leading the Global Talent Acquisition and Management team. Early in 2013, Kathleen was tasked with creating an integrated talent management organization that looks after the employee lifecycle. Prior to American Express, Kathleen acted as the global head of Talent Management and Acquisition at Thomson Reuters, having cut her teeth at both McKinsey and Bain.

Christy Mommsen joined American Express in 2013 as the director of Branding and Marketing Communication. She has overseen the relaunch of the global Careers website, now translated in seven languages and optimized for mobile technology. Christy holds an MBA from Columbia University and has lectured at both New York University and the University of Wisconsin. Prior to American Express, Christy worked in consumer marketing, most recently in the role of senior director of global marketing and new product innovation at Philips.

The journey for American Express began six years ago with a request to reimagine how the company went about talent acquisition. One of the most obvious issues was an outdated Careers website, which was suffering from aging and uninspiring visuals, as well as a clunky user experience. For example, when entering the site, only two options were provided for visitors to indicate where they lived, either within or outside of the United States. Such a binary choice did not reconcile with the diversity of regions where American Express operated and potentially left applicants wondering how seriously the company considered its overseas operations.

Yet, the Careers website was just the tip of the iceberg. A complete rethinking of the talent acquisition strategy was required. Kathleen encouraged the business to take a step back and consider the fundamentals of how American Express promoted itself to potential talent and the types of individuals the company targeted. She aspired to create an employer brand that would be on equal footing with its consumer brand. This was ambitious, to say the least, as American Express consistently ranks as one of the most well known and respected brands worldwide.

Until this point, talent acquisition at American Express was opportunistic. Strong talent in core business areas, such as marketing or consumer care, were naturally attracted to American Express and considered the company as a destination employer. When 2008 rolled around, this laissez-faire approach to recruiting was no longer sustainable. In the wake of the financial crisis, the CEO announced a change in corporate strategy to focus more heavily on digital payments, with direct implications for the type of talent that American Express needed to hire. Similar to the example of NPR earlier in this chapter, technology experts were in demand, but usually did not consider working for American Express. The stakes were high, as failing to create a new pipeline of talent would have direct implications for fulfilling the corporate strategy.

Taking stock of the work ahead of her, Kathleen recognized that the business needed to move away from either a geographic or business line approach to talent acquisition. Due to the underwhelming Careers website, a variety of recruiters set up their own landing pages to serve their local markets. Others took a different approach and focused on line of business. Although the job opportunities advertised might have made sense to internal talent, they had little chance of resonating with candidates outside of the company.

Kathleen's goal was to establish a "brand promise that would have relevance across geographies and business units," while providing a consistent experience for internal and external talent. Kathleen made the decision to embrace the company's heritage of what makes for a great consumer brand and apply it toward talent acquisition. Recognizing the power of the American Express brand, she knew that whatever employer brand they landed on would have to align to the larger organization.

Having worked in consumer marketing, Christy points out that "the process followed should be approximately the same for the two types of branding." The attention and rigor applied to the consumer brand should apply to the employer brand, especially when the stakes are high. She advises that a combination of qualitative, quantitative, and third-party research drives a holistic perspective. At American Express, Christy regularly consults trends in the consumer and employer brands, pulse surveys about employee sentiment (broken down by business unit, geography, and key talent), industry trends, and competitor analysis. She also conducts focus groups and interviews when new campaigns are launched.

Of the more notable trends uncovered recently by Christy is a disconnect between the public perception of American Express as an employer (specifically, that it provides a strong work-life balance) and the desires of high potentials already working within the company. Knowing that high potentials value meaningful work above work-life balance, she goes against the tide and actively sends messages about the quality of work to prospective employees. As a second example, she uncovered the fact that technology experts sometime misread and overlooked recruitment advertisements, failing to see the relevance for themselves in working at American Express.

The employer brand at American Express was defined as "Challenging Work with a Purpose" and is something that both Christy and Kathleen believe strongly that American Express can deliver on. Keeping true to this core brand, individual campaigns were launched to make the brand tangible and easy to understand. For example, a recent campaign titled *For Living* focused on the *purpose* component of the brand, headlining all the ways employees at American Express made a difference to their customers and the broader community. By focusing on the impact of their work, from protecting against fraud to delivering money thousands of miles away, employees demonstrated that their jobs had purpose. The campaign utilized a combination of videos and testimonials to make the content resonate with current and future employees.

In managing the employer brand, Christy segments her audiences, considering both the information they would like to receive and how they would like to receive it. As mentioned earlier, American Express is in the midst of a digital transformation that has required the company to compete for highly skilled technologists. To get potential applicants to take notice of American Express as an employer, a campaign titled *Powered by Innovation, Engineered by You* expresses what life is like as a technical expert at this particular time. Specifically, employees have a unique opportunity to create products and systems that will transform how payments are conducted, touching the lives of millions of customers globally.

Christy's goal was to ensure that the best technical talent recognized this opportunity and would seriously consider working for the company. By using a highly targeted campaign, Christy was careful not to compete against the "fundamental truth" about what it means to work at American Express. The campaign serves up plenty of *challenge* and *purpose*, acting as one translation of the employer brand.

Since 2006, American Express is reaping the benefits of a thoughtful and professional talent acquisition strategy. Although there is still work to be done for creating a healthy pipeline of highly sought-after talent, their employer brand has made them competitive against other destination employers. The magnitude of the change extends far beyond talent acquisition. Defining an employer brand helped

Kathleen express a unified vision for an integrated talent management strategy. Knowing what attracted and retained the best talent provided the groundwork for virtually all other talent management activities.

Key to the success of American Express was recognizing that talent acquisition could not be approached from a project perspective. To sustain the brand and ensure consistency, ongoing investment was required. Moreover, the approach taken mirrors the takeaways already identified in this chapter. Quantitative data was balanced with the qualitative in developing an EVP, while consistency was strived for across geographies and business units. Memorable campaigns that were extensions of the core brand, rather than competing against it, were created around authentic employee experiences to build transparency and trust.

Through their hard work and dedication, Kathleen and Christy have created an employer brand that meaningfully contributes to the reputation of American Express and complements its consumer brand. They have set a standard we should all aspire to.

# Chapter 3

## Capability Assessment

The act of selecting staff for recruitment or promotion is one of the hardest people decisions practitioners make. A choice is required based on who is most deserving for a job, resulting in both elation and disappointment, depending on which side of the fence the candidate is on. Usually, the ratio of jobs to candidates is not even and a far greater number of people will be disappointed. Depending on how invested emotionally and physically the candidates are in being hired, this disappointment can teeter on hatred for the hiring company. Sometimes, this feeling is warranted.

In a recent poll conducted in Australia, with over 1,000 candidates who had recently been through a hiring process, nearly 75 percent of candidates were dissatisfied with how they were treated by their prospective employers. More startling, a parallel study found that nearly 50 percent of candidates reported that they blamed the organization as a whole for their experience and their impression of the employer had been tarnished. So bad was this feeling that 18 percent would take their business elsewhere, 36 percent would complain to family and friends about the company, and 10 percent would engage in social media to expose their poor experience to strangers they don't even know.

These statistics beg the question: What is going on in the hiring process? Recruiters rushing the hiring process at the expense of a professional, systematic assessment surely is part of the problem, with candidates wondering why they would join a disorganized company that can't pull together a simple job interview. Justifiably, *candidate experience* has become a buzzword in the industry, and recruiters are now deeply aware that the employer brand must be managed all the way through the hiring process. Dim hallways leading onto a half-painted meeting room, with interviewers walking in ten minutes late with a stack of notes from previous candidates, does not make for the best impression and can undo all the good work in attracting the candidates to apply in the first place.

Candidate experience is only half of the story. Even when candidates go through a professional and clear-cut hiring process, they may feel that they were not given the opportunity to present themselves fully or that the recruiters were dead set against them from the start. These feelings are sometimes justified. Wrongful discrimination has occurred, either directly through interactions with the recruiter or indirectly through the criteria used for assessing which candidate was most appropriate for the job. Whether there was discrimination or not depends on the grounds upon which the hiring decision was made. If it was based on tangible skills and experience deemed necessary for the job, then the choice was sound. When based on assumptions, poor assessment methodology, or an inaccurate view of what the job entails, then wrongful discrimination has occurred, with potential legal ramifications.

Strong hiring decisions rely on both a clear understanding of what will be required on the job and the ability to accurately evaluate whether candidates have the potential to fulfill these responsibilities. In this chapter, I will discuss the latest thinking about how job profiles should be translated into assessment techniques, focusing on the difference between generic and job-specific forms of assessment. I will look at knowledge, skills, experience, and behavioral competency and whether there is a single best way of tapping into these characteristics as well as provide typical examples of assessment designs currently in use.

The relevance of generic cognitive ability (IQ or its derivatives) as a means of differentiating candidates for the modern workplace is questionable. I likewise challenge whether assessments can be used as a measure of future potential, as often done for selecting employees for talent management programs, or whether they should be confined as a rough guide to current capability. There is an amazing and diverse range of tools in the practitioner's toolbox for making selection decisions. In some ways, it is because of this choice that we fail to identify the right tool or place too much weight on one defining characteristic, resulting in our not choosing the most deserving talent.

## Evaluating Value and Risk

The role of assessor can be likened to any other job where the value and risk of a specific object must be judged. From the used car salesperson evaluating whether the bluebook value applies to a trade-in to a bank manager deciding whether to issue a small business loan, individuals are tasked with evaluating and judging what something is worth and whether there are any associated risks with a purchase.

Of the many analogies that can be made, consider a home inspector, whose decisions have the potential to crush or realize the dreams of first-time house buyers. As those of us who have had the joy of buying their first house can attest, a good survey can protect you from mold, insect infestations, subsidence, and a whole host of other issues that you have never even heard of. They are your last line of defense before putting your life's saving on the line. Whether you listen to your inspector is another story completely.

A good inspector will spend a considerable part of a day in careful observation, crawling into the depths of your potential new home, scrutinizing everything from the plumbing to the electricity. Based on their observations, they provide a professional opinion about the amount of risk that would be taken by a buyer, as well as evaluate the worth of the home. If major issues are discovered, buyers can use them to secure a lower price. If the risks are too high, buyers will simply walk away from the sale.

Inspectors go through significant training, have structured methodologies for ensuring all areas of a home are evaluated, and continuously learn about the latest trends in the housing market. Despite these assurances, the inspector cannot be 100 percent certain about his or her evaluation. Cracks behind built-in cabinets or leaks in pipes buried deep in the structure's foundation can go undetected. So the inspector's assessment is a best guess about the value of the home and its risks. The inspector's opinion, although not perfect, is better than that of a first-time buyer and, therefore, inspectors can charge significant fees for their work. They minimize the buying risk by applying professional training and practice.

To make the analogy back to hiring and promotion, assessors share the same responsibilities for evaluating value and risk. The recruiter scrutinizes the skills and experiences claimed by a candidate, using role profiles and organizational capability and competency frameworks as a guide. They dig deeper into the person's work history, through interviews and references, as a means of putting a value on the candidate's potential contribution to the business. Depending on the recruiters' sophistication, they may use business simulations, ability tests, or psychometrics to validate the candidate's work history and uncover risks. All this is done as a means of adding professionalism and structure to selection decisions.

Yet, unlike home inspectors, assessors are evaluating another living being who has a stake in his or her own evaluation. Candidates can be expected to sell their value and underplay any negatives, especially when they lack the opportunity to build rapport with the recruiter or when they are under significant pressure to secure employment. The job of an assessor is like that of a home inspector tasked with evaluating a house with all structural faults neatly tucked away behind the cabinetry.

Recent surveys confirm that candidate misrepresentation is common, with one-third of candidates admitting that they were dishonest during an interview. Seventeen percent of these candidates stretched the truth about their experience, 10 percent lied about their past salaries, 6 percent made up references, and 3 percent fabricated their qualifications. These findings are consistent with data from a similar study conducted five years ago with a pool of international job-seekers. Such dishonesty is not surprising to HR professionals. When polled, 95 percent of recruiters said they expect candidates to be dishonest and 55 percent have actually caught a candidate in the act through reference checks.

To guard themselves against misrepresentation and build a more accurate view of value and risk, organizations employ professional assessors trained in evaluating a candidate's fit to the job and organization. These individuals often sit within human resources, but increasingly are managers who hold assessment responsibilities along with their normal job duties. Organizational investment spans beyond resourcing assessors to include the tools and methodologies used by these professionals to improve the quality of their personnel decisions.

Two main criteria are used by assessors to evaluate how well any tool (such as an ability test) or methodology (made up of a series of business simulations or ability tests) is performing, specifically *reliability* and *validity*. Both criteria come in multiple forms. A brief description is provided below about how practitioners prove the worth of assessment. The topics of reliability and validity are of crucial importance to those of us put on the line to prove that wrongful discrimination has not occurred. From these two criteria you can decide how assessments should be used in your organization.

### FOUR FORMS OF RELIABILITY

Reliability refers to how consistently a tool or methodology differentiates between candidates of varying ability. For example, if a candidate took a numerical ability test and scored better than 70 percent of her peers, the test would be considered reliable if the same candidate scored close to her original score when retested (say in a range between 65 percent and 75 percent ). This form of reliability is called *test-retest reliability*. If looking across several assessments (ability tests or business simulations), reliability would be proven if the candidate consistently progresses to the same stage in the competition.

Most assessment tools are made up of a large number of questions, each contributing to the evaluation of some target ability. For example, a verbal reasoning test evaluates a candidate's comprehension of a series of written passages. The measure of how well the questions related to each passage contribute to the overall assessment of verbal reasoning is called *internal consistency reliability*. If an individual item causes confusion among respondents or is not related to how candidates complete the remainder of the assessment, the item should be removed from the test battery.

The two remaining forms of reliability take on importance depending on the assessment design. *Inter-rater reliability* should be checked when two or more assessors are used simultaneously in the selection process. By comparing how each assessor evaluates the same candidate, reliability can be proven and the assessors allowed to evaluate candidates on their own. *Parallel-forms reliability* applies to situations when candidates may undergo assessment repetitively, for example, when reapplying for promotion after a failed first attempt. Two or more versions of the test can be built to evaluate the same construct, but with distinct items to eliminate bias.

An assessment must prove it is reliable before its benefits can be evaluated. Unreliable results cannot be used to discriminate between candidates, as the relationship between the test and job performance would be tenuous. If a tool or methodology has been shown to be reliable through the four types of reliability (test-retest, internal consistency, inter-rater, and parallel forms), then the worth of the assessment can be judged, defined as its *validity*.

### THREE FORMS OF VALIDITY

There are three main types of validity (*content, construct,* and *criterion*), and each helps prove the value that any assessment tool or process brings to selection decisions. The first type of validity—*content validity*—is how well the assessment looks and feels like the target skill. For example, if an ability test is said to measure mathematical skill, the content of the test will most likely include questions involving adding, subtracting, multiplying, and dividing a wide range of numbers. On first glance, such a test would look like it measures the right skill (referred to as *face validity*) and is related to the construct (called *representation validity*), as mathematical ability is defined by the ability to perform such calculations.

Content validity is particularly important for the modern workplace, as poorly administered tests may be measuring skills that bear little or no relation to the intended target. For example, verbal reasoning tests rely on a high level of language mastery and, therefore, may be measuring how fluent a candidate is in the language, rather than his or her actual critical reasoning skill. It is not surprising that candidates show lower verbal reasoning skills when they are tested outside their mother tongues.

The second major form—*construct validity*—looks at the comparison between a given assessment and other measurements. Assessments that are said to measure the same target (such as mathematical skill) should be highly correlated with each other (referred to as *convergent validity*), whereas unrelated measures (such as mathematical and typing skills) should be found different when candidate scores are compared (referred to as *divergent validity*).

The third form of validity—*criterion validity*—is really what business people are after; the ability to predict tangible results in the workplace. Criterion validity summarizes the assessment's relationship to employee engagement, satisfaction, behavior, or performance, either now (termed *concurrent validity*) or in the future (called *predictive validity*). The quest for criterion validity is the holy grail of the assessment world, as those responsible for selection are increasingly challenged to demonstrate the value of expensive applicant tracking and assessment systems.

In many ways, this quest falls flat. To prove the value of an assessment, occupational psychologists often point to a series of meta analyses that have compared the relative worth of different selection tools to job performance. These studies have found that a combination of tools works best to predict performance, beyond the single use of any given measure. Moreover, demographics such as age or years of experience were not found to be significantly related to performance, providing additional support for policies promoting equality in the workplace. Despite their widespread use, employer references were found to be ineffectual at predicting performance, due in part to the candidate's ability to control who acts as a reference, as well as an increasing reluctance by employers to provide information beyond length of service or job title, for fear of legal backlash. Types of reliability and validity are summarized in Figure 3.1.

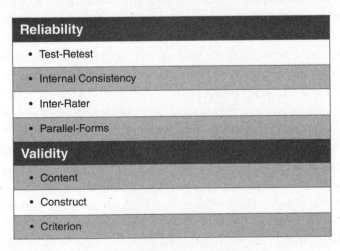

| Reliability |
| --- |
| • Test-Retest |
| • Internal Consistency |
| • Inter-Rater |
| • Parallel-Forms |

| Validity |
| --- |
| • Content |
| • Construct |
| • Criterion |

FIGURE 3.1  Summary of Types of Reliability and Validity

Individual forms of assessment, such as a structured interview, ability test, situational judgment test, or psychometric, perform better than doing nothing at all, with correlations ranging between 0.40 and 0.55. For those unfamiliar with statistics, a correlation of 0 represents no relationship between variables, whereas a value of 1.00 would represent an assessment tool that could perfectly predict performance. Research found that a combination of assessment tools, for example, an ability test and a structured interview, improve the correlation coefficient to nearly 0.65.

On the face of it, this is a good result. Assessments significantly predict performance, while demographic characteristics have been discredited, to the chagrin of bigots everywhere. Yet, a 0.65 correlation means that only 42 percent of a candidate's performance can be accurately predicted by assessment. In other words, there is more that is unknown about a particular employee's potential to perform than is known. Workplace culture, relationships with managers and co-workers, distribution of responsibilities, on-the-job training, the economic environment, and pure chance all play a part in how well an employee performs on the job.

To make matters worse, the statistics provided represent active research into the relationship between assessment and performance, where variables are carefully selected and pursued. For the majority of organizations, the availability of good quality assessment and performance data is extremely limited. Inconsistencies in assessment methodology, missing candidate records, poor performance data, and a lack of statistical know-how all contribute to uncertainty about how effective any assessment regime can be. Less than perfect implementation of an assessment regime will likely result in lower predictive ability than that reported here.

Until recently, there has been a lack of desire among businesses to prove the worth of their assessments. Hiring managers took it for granted that assessment tools could identify the right candidates, often paying premium fees for expert opinions about a candidate's worth. With the recent global financial crisis, this has changed and business leaders are demanding that their investment in human resources systems result in tangible benefits, such as greater employee productivity, increased revenue, and cost savings. With a lack of information and a general inability to analyze it, conversations about return on investment prove frustrating to human resource and business leaders alike, due to the complexity of identifying, tracking, and analyzing the data.

This discussion has adopted a single perspective for evaluating the worth of assessment, specifically how job and organizational performance can be improved by correctly identifying capability. Other perspectives on the value of assessment are receiving increased amounts of attention by recruiters. Specifically, the subjective opinions of both managers and candidates are entering into the discussion. For managers, recruiters are asking how satisfied they are with recent appointments, as well as perceptions about candidates' progress during induction, and training post-appointment. For candidates, information is captured on the recruitment process and how well aligned it is to the employer brand, as well as ongoing engagement resulting from the fulfillment of expectations or lack thereof.

Where does that leave us? At a broad level, assessment appears to be a worthwhile activity, as a means of vetting capability and allowing a way to choose among candidates. In comparison to demographic information, graphology, or informal conversations with prospective employees, assessment appears to provide credible information about a candidate's ability. When used with résumé screening and an evaluation of candidate motivation, employer confidence can be built around hiring or promotion decisions.

For these reasons, assessment is the norm for the majority of organizations. In a poll conducted in March 2011 of 463 human resource executives in eight countries and representing eighteen industries, 80 percent of respondents reported using structured interviews (27 percent over the web), 78 percent use application forms that target key skills and experience, 65 percent use structured phone screens, and 51 percent conduct assessment centers that involve a combination of simulations, ability tests, and psychometrics. Taken on their own, these actions speak volumes for the acceptance of assessment in recruitment and promotion.

However, there is room for improvement, as assessment techniques are only partially predicting performance. Factors outside the control of recruiters interfere with the relationship between assessment and performance once an employee is on the job. Moreover, organizations must be mindful of their assessment practices to ensure they make the most of the information gathered during the hiring or promotion process.

In the following section, we look at what is legally required of employers when making hiring or promotion decisions, before we look at the specific tools and techniques used to ensure compliance. The discussion sets out the minimum requirements of employers, without asking what else could be done to promote an excellent candidate experience or a cutting-edge process for identifying top talent.

## Legal Requirements

I will focus on one specific legal system to frame what is required of employers in making hiring or promotion decisions; one that I have intimate knowledge of as a practitioner. The principles of Australia's framework have similarity to those of other countries I have worked in (including the United States, the UK, and Ireland), focusing on protecting employee rights and ensuring that wrongful discrimination does not occur. For an excellent review of the commonalities across various legal systems, see Brett Myors' paper, "International Perspectives on the Legal Environment for Selection" (2008).

The most recent piece of legislation governing workplace practices is the Fair Work Act 2009, wherein three independent bodies were set up to protect the basic rights of people working in Australia. These bodies include the Fair Work Ombudsman, Fair Work Australia, and Fair Work Divisions of the Federal Court and the Federal Magistrates Court. In particular, the Fair Work Ombudsman is empowered to provide education and assistance on workplace law, promote and monitor compliance, investigate any act or practice that runs contrary to the law, seek penalties where a breach has occurred, and represent employees or outworkers when necessary.

The Fair Work Act 2009 sets out that unlawful discrimination occurs when an employer takes adverse action against an individual based on race, color, sex, sexual preference, age, physical or mental disability, marital status, family or career responsibilities, pregnancy, religion, political opinion, or social origin. The law applies to the full range of employees (full-time, casual, apprentices, etc.) and protects against employers making unfair decisions (or failures to accommodate) regarding dismissal, pay, contractual arrangements, and hiring.

As set out in the Act, it is lawful to treat employees differently, as long as it is not due to the personal attributes set out above. A simple example of this is when an employee's performance is substandard and he or she is denied a pay increase. In some instances, the inherent requirements of the job may call for an employee to be treated differently (for example, offering employment based on how much an individual can physically lift). Under the law, a penalty of $33,000 per contravention, per corporation can be charged. The courts can also order injunctions, reinstatement, and/or compensation to the affected employee.

To assist employers to meet the requirements of the Act, the Fair Work Ombudsman, in conjunction with the Victorian Equal Opportunity and Human Rights Commission, outlines practices that employers should adhere to. When advertising a position, focus should be placed on essential skills and experience, while avoiding reference to age, sex, race, or other personal characteristics. The advertisements should be written in a way that attracts a diverse range of suitable candidates and does not discourage specific audiences from applying. When working with recruitment agencies, employers are responsible for providing a clear brief and ensuring that the agency is up-to-date on anti-discrimination laws.

The application process should be open and accessible. For example, paper applications should be accepted alongside electronic applications, so as not to discourage candidates without access to computers. When invited for an interview, candidates should be asked about any special requirements that they have, while the venue itself should be wheelchair-accessible.

When conducting interviews, employers cannot request information about a person's background and refuse a job based on this information. Candidates are not obligated to disclose information about disability or illness unless it is relevant to the job. Employers are encouraged to use a common interview structure and scoring system that is applied to all candidates. The interviewers themselves should be well briefed on the job and aware of anti-discrimination laws. Where possible, a diverse range of interviewers should be used on the selection panel.

If psychometric tests are used, they should relate directly to the requirements of the job, assessing a candidate's suitability based on specific selection criteria. Employers are tasked with ensuring that the aptitude test is appropriate for the role and does not discriminate against people with a disability or from a different cultural background. The results should be interpreted by an expert and combined with other sources of information about a candidate.

Decisions should be based on demonstrated skills and abilities, accessing the full range of information collected about a candidate (interview notes, referee reports, résumé, etc.). Ranking should occur based on what is essential for job performance, with a written record kept of the rationale behind the selection decision. The process should be kept confidential and assessment materials securely stored.

In sum, the law sets out what employers cannot do, specifically, making decisions based on personal attributes that have no relation to the job. The recommendations made by government agencies provide guidance about how employers can safeguard themselves and promote equality in the workplace. However, there is still a great deal of latitude in what practices employers can adopt, while some employers choose to ignore the law completely. As you read through the sections below, it may be helpful to reference what is required by the law, alongside arguments about reliability and validity, to judge the different types of assessments.

## Assessment by Interview

Across cultures and industries, interviews are the most common way to assess candidate ability, providing a means of exploring their work history and validating both the breadth and depth of their experience. The Chartered Institute of Personnel Development (CIPD) provides a snapshot of how often two main types of interviews are used by companies. In 2004, *biographical interviews* exploring the candidate's skills or work history were used in 66 percent of all hiring situations. Biographical interviews are based on the premise that past performance (what has been accomplished in previous roles) will predict future success.

The second type of interview, *competency-based interviews,* focus on behavioral frameworks about how an individual should work with his or her colleagues, suppliers, partners, or customers (see Figure 3.2).

| A. **Give me an example of a time when you had to satisfy a particular customer need (either internal or external).**<br>• How did you establish what the customer's needs were?<br>• What steps did you take to ensure that the customer was fully satisfied with your work?<br>• How effectively did you satisfy the customer's expectations?<br>• What would you have done differently? | **Example Behavior:**<br>□ Develops a clear understanding of the customer's business<br>□ Proactively identifies customer requirements, expectations, and needs<br>□ Seeks customer feedback and ensures that customer issues are effectively resolved<br>□ Looks for ways to improve processes for the benefit of the customer |
|---|---|
| B. **Give me an example of a time when you were responsible for delivering an important project.**<br>• How did you ensure that others delivered the work you needed?<br>• How did you personally ensure that the work delivered was of the required standard?<br>• How did you resolve any issues you faced?<br>• What would you have done differently? | □ Takes responsibility for own work<br>□ Takes responsibility for work of others<br>□ Takes immediate action if required<br>□ Delivers on commitments |
| | **TOTAL SCORE** |

FIGURE **3.2** Example of a Competency-Based Interview for Customer Service

The Chartered Institute of Personnel Development found that competency-based interviews were used in 62 percent of cases. Unlike the biographical interview, which focuses on "what" someone has accomplished, the competency-based interview explores "how" someone goes about his or her job. These two formats, technically and behaviorally driven, are complementary in scope and are normally used together in hiring or promotion decisions.

Beyond type of interview, there is a great deal of variety in how many interviews are typically experienced by candidates. A survey of UK practices in 1991 found that the majority of candidates experience multiple rounds of interviews, with nearly 49 percent experiencing two interviews, 26 percent experiencing three interviews, and an unlucky 11 percent having to undergo four or more rounds of interviews. The same survey found that panels (more than one interviewer) are used frequently, with two interviewers questioning 40 percent of candidates, three interviewers grilling 35 percent of candidates, and four or more interviewers badgering 19 percent of candidates. An international survey conducted in 2011 found that panels involving at least two assessors are now used in 73 percent of interviews. These statistics reveal that organizations invest a great deal of time and energy into interviews. The question is, To what end?

The desired benefits go beyond validating candidate ability by providing an opportunity for hiring managers to meet prospective employees and evaluate fit. Until the interview stage, recruiters may have been entirely responsible for screening and short-listing candidates, especially in large organizations. The communication gap between recruiters and line managers closes as soon as a job candidate is invited for an interview. Interviews can also benefit candidates by creating a platform for them to evaluate their own fit to the hiring manager and workplace. As they learn more about the job opening, skilled candidates might begin to have second thoughts if the manager or workplace fails to deliver on the image projected in the job advertisement. The interview is a window into the organization and, through it, candidates glimpse what life would look like if they accepted the job.

At their best, interviews are a two-way process, where employers and candidates size each other up and evaluate whether there is enough common ground to consider a formalized working relationship. The real question is how often and under what conditions interviews live up to their promise. Should interviews continue to be the leading means of making selection decisions?

Just looking at the hard statistics, interviews are not terribly effective at predicting job success, despite their prevalence, even when highly structured and based on known job requirements. Interviews account for only 20 percent of a candidate's job performance, whereas unstructured versions, with poor structure and inconsistencies in administration between candidates (unfortunately, the more common type), perform only marginally better than pure chance.

At the most basic level, part of their inaccuracy is a function of self-report. Candidates are talking about their experience in their own words. Negative traits must be inferred by assessors, either through inconsistencies or omission of facts. Returning to our analogy of the home inspector, an interview would be analogous to asking the seller about potential flaws in the house without doing a physical inspection. Just like a job candidate, the seller is not incentivized to tell you anything about the house that would raise suspicion or make you doubt the purchase. The seller is not likely to tell you about the hole in the roof or the family of cockroaches living under the floorboards. Thus, interviewers must satisfy themselves that any information gleaned from interviews will differentiate candidates only by their positive qualities and the depth and breadth of their experience, rather than their failure to perform.

The other reason for their poor predictability lies with the interviewer and how much rigor he or she puts toward conducting the interview. Whether the interview is biographical or competency-based, conducted one-to-one or with a panel, or done in a series or as a stand-alone, human error creeps into the process and biases selection decisions. Practitioners cannot do anything about the problem of false self-report, but are obligated to maintain the rigor of the interview process.

With this in mind, below are the top five ways interviews go wrong, with a few real examples of bad practice from my own career. I also point out some key lessons along the way.

### SNAP JUDGMENTS

I have heard excuse after excuse about why managers fail to adopt a formalized interview process. "I can spot them at a distance," "I trust my gut instinct," or "I'm a great judge of character" have all been used on me. The truth is that managers do trust their instincts and do make snap judgments that shape the way the interview is conducted, causing their initial impression to be correct. If a manager takes a shine to a candidate, the remainder of the interview time is spent confirming initial judgments, usually ending in a job offer.

Startling research conducted by Tricia Prickett discovered that as little as fifteen seconds, the time required to knock on the door and shake hands, was enough for judgments to be made about a candidate's capability. In her research, an independent party watched footage of a candidate interacting with an interviewer. From this fifteen seconds of tape, the observers were able to accurately predict how the interviewer rated nine out of eleven personal traits. What's happening here? Can we all spot those high prospect employees, who exude confidence, initiative, and are likely to be asset to any organization?

The truth is more sinister, in that both the interviewer's and third party's judgments are biased, setting in motion a self-fulfilling prophecy. The power of that initial fifteen seconds tainted both their views of the candidate, leading to an assumption of capability. Although the observer stopped watching the footage, the interview went on with questions that reaffirmed the interviewer's initial judgments, assuring that his or her ratings would be aligned to those of the third-party observer.

Those who have a firm handshake, speak with confidence, and look professional use snap judgments to their benefit. For those lacking confidence or who happen to come from a nontraditional or minority background can attest, snap judgments are a constant worry. Research on stereotypes has demonstrated that people generally tend to reaffirm their views about group differences and, as a result, make decisions that preserve their assumptions about who is most appropriate for a given job.

## Placing Blame

Psychologists have long been interested in the "fundamental attribution error," a technical way of saying that individuals are sometimes blamed for things outside of their control. In general, Western cultures place an inordinate amount of emphasis on inherent traits, downplaying social context or luck. Early research by Newcomb in the 1920s questioned whether extraversion is an inherent trait, whereby behaviors exhibited in one social gathering would predict the amount of extraversion among boys in a summer camp.

Interestingly, when a novel social situation was encountered by the boys, predictions about extraversion did not hold. Boys labeled as extroverted would not always speak up, while the quiet boys often came into their own when a new social context was presented. Believing that the inherent personality trait of extraversion will dominate all social contexts is a demonstration of the fundamental attribution error. More recent examples include research by Mischel and Peake at Carleton College, where behaviors involving cleanliness and punctuality failed to transfer between contexts. Just because your roommate may leave empty pizza boxes on the bedroom floor does not necessarily mean that he or she will do the same at work.

As applied to the interview context, employers assume that good or bad performance in one job will apply to the next. Such an assumption discounts the role that the previous company's culture, systems, and co-workers played in the candidate's success on the job. Even fate may have been in their favor, with customers beating down the door or a string of lucky breaks that resulted in an impressive track record of performance. On the flip side, employers make assumptions that poor interview responses indicate a questionable future for job candidates. Either way, interpreting interview data can lead to the fundamental attribution error and a bad hiring decision.

## POINT OF COMPARISON

It is rare that only one candidate is interviewed for a job. From my experience, shortlists are usually made up of three suitably qualified candidates, who are then brought to a final interview. Based on where these candidates are from (either internal or external to the company) and in which order they are interviewed, bias can creep in.

More is known about *internal* candidates. Their performance in the workplace, attitudes toward work, and social networks are generally common knowledge to hiring managers. Whether this benefits the internal candidate depends on his or her reputation, whereas information about external candidates comes almost entirely from the assessment process (although recruiters have been known to "google" a candidate or two). I have personally witnessed hiring managers adding their own interpretations to an internal candidate's answer to an interview question, documenting how it "really went down." To combat against bias shown toward internal candidates, recruiters often involve independent third parties or managers who have had little interaction with the employees.

The order of interview candidates also affects how successful they will be in receiving a job offer. A really good or bad candidate at the beginning of the day may taint how the others are viewed. Candidates going after lunch may find their interviewers lacking in energy and may find it difficult to connect with them. In a recent restructuring project, I conducted back-to-back interviews for three weeks solid, all for the same role. After completing more than seventy interviews using the same twelve questions, exhaustion was inevitable, especially as my candidates (all from the same company) used nearly the same examples to demonstrate their capability.

## CHEMISTRY

Early in my own career, I tried for a job with a management consultancy firm. The process was a lengthy one, with a series of phone interviews and a trip to San Francisco for a day of assessment and face-to-face interviews. After six grueling hours, I met with a partner from the firm. I knew from the moment that I entered her office that I would not land the job. Plainly put, we had the wrong chemistry. The interview itself wasn't horrible; all the pieces were there, including a review of my experience, what I wanted out of the job, and so forth.

The conversation was simply flat and, being with the managing partner, the interview was decisive in my rejection from the competition. Looking back, this was not a bad outcome. I would have had a different career path if I had taken that job and would likely have missed out on finding the field of occupational psychology. But I think about how much time was wasted on both sides due to a hiring process that ended because of a mismatch in personality.

Sometimes we, as candidates, get it wrong. My wife had an interview with an organization and met me in a coffee shop directly afterward. She was convinced that the interview was a flop due to her chemistry with the interviewers. In fact, she completely misread the interviewers' signals, having interpreted their hesitation as a negative instead of recognizing that they were trying to find a way of adapting the role to meet her capabilities. She was too qualified for the role, and they knew that the role would have to change if they wanted to hire her.

Interviewers prefer candidates who are like themselves. When asked about how their preferences influence their hiring decisions, interviewers report that 80 percent of candidates they personally liked were offered jobs, compared to only 40 percent of candidates where the chemistry was poor. These decisions have nothing to do with capability or willingness to do the job. If the hiring manager is doing the interviews, this preference may be warranted, as the manager will have to deal with the consequences of any disagreement in working style. However, such bias is likely to lead to homogenous teams, which often succumb to groupthink and lack of healthy challenge.

## ONE RATING

Hiring is a yes-or-no decision. Either the candidate passes the assessment and is offered a job or he or she is released from the competition. Even when a merit list is prepared because multiple positions are open, with candidates ranked according to their fit for the job, an assessment process must result in a tangible recommendation about who to hire. In such cases, I generally recommend that a cutoff be used, below which unsuitable candidates are released from the hiring process without being ranked on a merit list.

Coming to an overall score and recommendation can be a tricky process. Interviews gather a wide range of information across multiple areas of experience. How an assessor weighs this information and distills it down to a single score is often more art than science. Bias creeps in, especially when an interviewer's ratings are compared with those of his or her peers. When interviewers are studied side-by-side, one interviewer may focus on and weigh an interview response more heavily than the other interviewer, discounting examples given earlier or later in the interview.

Without a proper briefing about the job and its requirements, interviewers tend to hold different views of what "good" looks like and, because of this, hold candidates accountable to inconsistent standards. Interviewers may also bring their own career biases into the interview. For example, how an interviewer weighs the relative importance of on-the-job experience against formalized education can change how questions are phrased and where emphasis is placed when exploring a candidate's résumé.

The difficulty of coming to a single and definitive evaluation of candidate suitability is most dramatic in panels, where issues of favoritism and bias are played out in a public setting. Panel interviews are very much a special case, where organizational pressures around hierarchy (whose opinions matter most), competing interests (how the candidate's time will be used), and future strategy (which candidate will be best aligned) can interfere with an objective evaluation of candidates, especially when a clear structure or chairperson is missing. I once was interviewed by an academic interview panel where seven department members were involved in the selection decision. Despite a strong chairperson, it was obvious to me that some members were disinterested in the exercise and others were biting their tongues.

In the discussion above, I have shown that interviews can and often do go wrong. The bias created by instantaneous judgments of candidates, our inferences about causes for interview responses, the comparisons we make between candidates, the chemistry we experience, and how we weigh information to decide on an overall score all challenge the reliability and validity of interviews as a worthwhile assessment technique. Below are a few recommendations about how interviews could be improved. Even if these were strictly followed, I believe that the interview will always be limited in its ability to differentiate correctly between candidates.

- ◆ *Structure the interview.* To ensure that each candidate has an equal opportunity to prove his or her capability, the same list of topics should be explored in the interview (whether biographical or competency-based) and in the same order. Generally speaking, each topic should have a leading open-ended question asking about experience, followed by three or more probing questions. Alternative questions can be provided (useful for when an example does not come quickly to the candidate's mind), as long as the questions have been proven to evaluate the same target. Suitable time should be given for each topic, with ten or fifteen minutes being the norm. When done right, improving the structure increases both reliability (internal consistency and parallel forms) and content validity.

- ◆ *Train the interviewers.* Whether interviewers follow the new structure depends on how well they have been trained. Explaining how bias can creep into the interview, the necessity of providing equal time and asking the same questions to each candidate, and the need to take accurate notes throughout go a long way to improve the reliability (inter-rater) of the interview. Moreover, discussing how the questions asked during interviews relate to success on the job can help interviewers agree on what "good" looks like and to focus on information that directly addresses a candidate's fit for the job. Using video footage or role plays that target what information should be used to make a hiring decision can instill consistency across assessors.

♦ ***Compare the technique.*** The only way to prove the worth of any interview design is to study how well candidate responses are related to other forms of assessment, geared to evaluate the same criteria and performance outcomes on the job. Such research provides confidence around the content and criterion validity of the technique and, therefore, should be sought out when large-scale recruitment or promotion activities are undertaken.

## Knowledge, Skills, and Abilities

If we return to our home inspector analogy, our faithful inspector has just finished a conversation with the current owners about the benefits of the house. On occasion, the inspector may have politely asked the owners about any issues they are experiencing with the house, but this was not the focus of the conversation. The information our inspector gained confirmed what was expected: the house has four bedrooms, a modernized kitchen, and it ranks high in energy efficiency. Any building issues from the last five years have already been resolved, and there is no major work required at this time. By the way, the neighbors are a pleasure and have never complained about noise, even after the New Year's Eve party that has been called legendary by all your friends. In essence, the house is a bargain by any definition.

But our inspector is no fool. The condition and building standards of the house must be tested, before the buyers can be given the all clear. The home inspector will visit the property, measuring and documenting everything that can be seen and experienced. From the plumbing to the electric, the house will be scrutinized and a report drafted about how well the house meets the asking price. If more specialist advice is needed, the inspector may recommend a second visit or a quote from a tradesperson. From there, the decision is up to the buyers whether they would like to complete the sale.

Bringing the analogy back to the workplace, interviews and reference checks accomplish only so much in validating a candidate's capability. Assessments targeting knowledge, skills, and ability go to the heart of what a candidate has to offer. Such assessments allow for comparisons among candidates, allowing employers to rank-order individuals who passed a minimal level of capability.

The differences among knowledge, skills, and abilities are hard to define, and there is significant overlap between the terms. In general, *knowledge* questions whether a candidate is aware of a given topic, whereas *skills* ask whether the candidate can put this knowledge to use. An *ability* is a higher order concept, questioning whether a candidate can apply his or her skills across a variety of contexts or problems.

The most prolific way for assessing knowledge, skills, and ability is to review a candidate's résumé. Formalized education and industry or geographical experience all provide an indication about whether the candidate has the right level of knowledge. Similarly, skills can be assessed by looking at the attainment of formalized training, memberships to professional bodies where continuous professional development is required, and other forms of professional certification. Ability is not usually captured on a résumé; unless a candidate reports the scores used for selection into postgraduate education, for instance.

Employers often want to validate what a candidate has claimed on his or her résumé and turn to the world of occupational psychology for help. Occupational psychologists have had a long history of grappling with exactly what can be gained through testing, how relevant it is to work, and what it all means. In fact, it is estimated that as much as 70 percent of organizations use knowledge, skills, or ability testing in their recruitment process. In this section, I will provide a brief history of testing, the evolution of IQ as a concept, and the legacy of tools (both good and bad) that are currently available to practitioners.

### The Quest for General Intelligence

Wouldn't it be great to find a single system for ranking capability and potential among individuals, whether for educational or employment purposes? Think of all the time and energy that could be saved by investing in the right type of person, rather than investing in everybody. As long as the right person could be spotted early, the benefits would be enormous, as training and experiential opportunities could be directed to those who would gain the most. But what about the societal consequences of such a scheme? What exactly would be measured? How can you ensure that everyone has a fair chance? And what happens if a person scores poorly? Can the person retake the test or prove his or her worth in an alternative way?

This is the essence of the debate on IQ. In individualistic societies, there is a natural tendency to find and label individuals according to their potential to succeed in school and work. Psychologists have fostered this world view through the promotion of the measurement of individual differences and their desire to provide information that is relevant for society. To see just how far the notion of IQ extends in our vernacular, take a moment to reflect on examples from the popular media (with quiz shows either directly or indirectly referencing a player's intellect) or from your own social interactions (when we comment on how clever someone is). Few people recognize that the words *idiot, imbecile,* and *moron* were previously scientific words related to degrees of retardation (mental ages of two years, three to seven years, and eight to twelve years, respectively). Not everyone buys into a singular view of intelligence, arguing that the damage caused by this view outweighs any tangible benefits from labeling and ranking people by IQ.

The history of IQ starts with a variety of now defunct theories of mind that set the stage for how IQ was positioned with psychologists and the general public. Three fads from the 19th century deserve special mention, specifically Craniometry (Figures 3.3 and 3.4), Recapitulation (Figures 3.5 and 3.6), and Apish Morphology (Figure 3.5). Craniometry held that the size of a person's head was directly related to intelligence (even Francis Galton was fascinated by stuffing marbles into skulls), whereas Recapitulation focused on the development of the human embryo and how it revealed our animal origins. Apish Morphology focused on proving that criminals share a common look, which, if spotted early, could help in the prevention of crime (different crimes even had their own stereotypes, focusing on facial features like the size of one's jaw or the narrowness of a person's eyes). Together, these fads set in motion a belief system that intelligence could be recognized, measured, and ranked for the betterment of society.

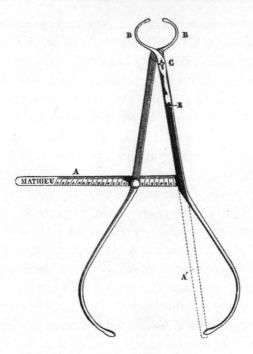

FIGURE **3.3**  Image of Calipers Used for Craniometry
*Source:* Wellcome Library, London. Used with permission.

The first standardized test of generalized intelligence is usually attributed to Binet. On closer examination, what Binet was tasked to do bears little resemblance to the modern concept of IQ, making me wonder if he turns in his grave every time the UK TV show *Test the Nation* is aired. Far from looking at what constitutes genius, Binet was originally tasked by the French government with creating a tool that could identify children with learning disabilities. Using short individual modules containing every type of test Binet could think of, children were classified by their mental age (how well they scored as compared to children of different chronological ages). In the words of Binet, "It matters very little what the tests are so long as they are numerous."

In building his tests, Binet held to three principles. First, the tests had to be practical. The scores themselves did not in any way support a theory of intellect. Second, the scale was a rough tool for

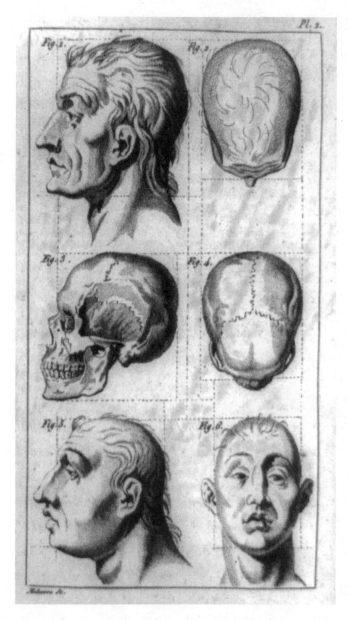

FIGURE 3.4 Image of a Comparison Between Two Men, One Sane and the Other Insane, in the Cranial Shapes of Their Skulls

*Source:* The tradition of science/Leonard C. Bruno. Washington, DC: Library of Congress, 1987, p. 158. Used with permission.

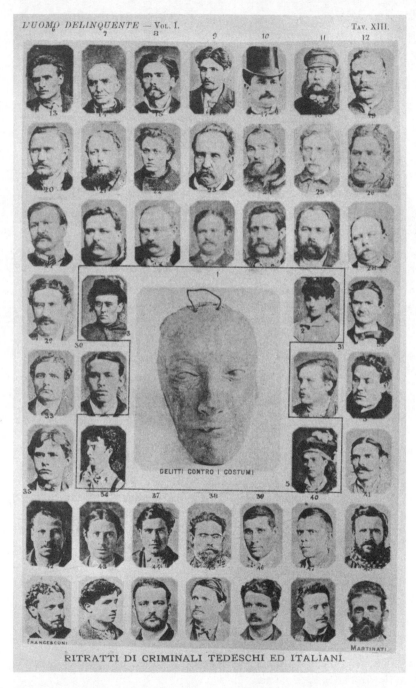

RITRATTI DI CRIMINALI TEDESCHI ED ITALIANI.

FIGURE 3.5   Image of Seventeen Known Criminals

*Source:* Wellcome Library, London. Used with permission.

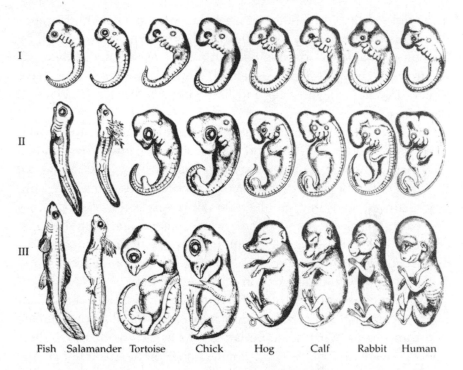

Fish  Salamander  Tortoise  Chick  Hog  Calf  Rabbit  Human

FIGURE **3.6** Comparison Among Embryos to Illustrate Recapitulation

*Source:* Wikimedia Commons, the free media repository.

identifying children as retarded or having learning disabilities. It was not intended to differentiate among "normal" children. Third, whatever an individual's score, test findings should be used to determine how improvement could occur through special education.

Unfortunately, it did not take long for Binet's test to be misconstrued into its present format. Shortly after the turn of the century and with advent of World War I, practitioners latched onto IQ as a quick way of allocating professions and determining who received opportunities for further education. These practitioners assumed that intelligence was innate and inherited, could be measured by a single score (IQ), and would remain stable across an individual's life.

In a highly recommended book about the history of IQ, Gould in *Mismeasure of Man* (1996) states that current notions of IQ are fundamentally flawed. He alleges that IQ is reductionist, in that it oversimplifies complex human ability and has become reified into a tangible entity from little or no basis. Moreover, Gould argues that IQ is discriminatory at both an individual and group level, by attaching a value to how high-scoring and low-scoring individuals are treated. Group differences across ethnic and gender lines have fueled arguments against IQ and its legitimacy for use in selection decisions.

Since Gould, the debate rages on. Of the recent authors who have spoken out against IQ and its correlates, Gladwell has studied the origins of talent. Unlike most accounts of genius that talk about the unique combination of intellectual power, obsession, and epiphany, Gladwell notes that simultaneous discovery is the norm and not the exception. Newton and Leibniz were contemporaries in their discovery of calculus, as were Darwin and Wallace with evolution, Cros and Ducos du Hauron in the development of color photographs, and Bell and Grey with the invention of the telephone.

Such multiple origins of discovery tell us that many of humankind's greatest achievements are inevitable and a product of a climate of advancement. What does predict genius is hard work and dedication. Gladwell in *Outliers* (2008) makes note of the 10,000-hour rule of effortful practice that, along with being in the right place at the right time, allows individuals to do great things. Each genius plays a part by improving his or her ability to perform, but context determines whether there is access to specialist equipment, a teacher who can provide the right level of support and challenge, and an opportunity to perform. This combination of practice and context applies across professional fields, from artistic greats like the Beatles to industry leaders in technology, including Bill Gates, Bill Joy, and the late Steve Jobs.

The world of business has been slow to abandon its fascination with innate talent. Trends in CEO compensation attest to an underlying belief in the superiority of individual contribution over the effects of social or environmental influences on business performance. In 1999, CEOs were paid on average $11.9 million a year, according to the AFL-CIO (2000). However, pay levels vary dramatically across cultures, with individualistic cultures paying more than collectivist cultures. The disparity between CEOs and their lowest paid worker is 476 times greater in the United States, compared to thirteen times greater in Germany, and eleven times greater in Japan.

The difference in pay accelerated greatly in the 1980s and 1990s in the United States, from forty-two times in 1980 to eighty-five times in 1990, and finally to 476 by the end of the millennium. All the while, researchers have been looking at the relationship between innate talent and business performance, discovering that the correlation (although statistically significant) is low at approximately .20. Despite industry's desire to recruit and incentivize the best leadership talent, CEOs may not be able to replicate their performance in a new organization. Sometimes, the context is wrong and, at other times, their initial success was simply due to chance.

## TYPES OF ABILITY

When looking across the field of assessment, differentiated ability is the rule rather than the exception. From a legal perspective, ability tests that are directly linked to job responsibilities are more defensible than a general intelligence score that is said to apply universally to all roles. Line and business managers often require this link, too, if they are to buy into any large-scale assessment regime that is said to produce more capable workers specific to their areas of responsibility.

A wide array of models of differentiated ability have been positioned as a counterpoint to IQ. Notably, Gardner proposed that seven main types of intelligence exist: linguistic, logical-mathematical, musical, bodily kinesthetic, spatial, interpersonal, and intra-personal types. As an alternative model, Sternberg suggests that there are three core types of intelligence that lead to success in life: analytic (the ability to solve problems), creative (deciding what problems to solve), and practical (devising effective solutions).

As applied to the current field of occupational psychology, I routinely come across eight main types of ability tests:

- ◆ ***Verbal reasoning:*** Following the logic of written passages and making decisions based on their content.
- ◆ ***Numerical reasoning:*** Working with numerical and statistical information to make inferences about trends.
- ◆ ***Inductive reasoning:*** Establishing rules from a series of shapes and applying the rule to identify the next item in the series.

- ◆ *Deductive reasoning:* Using established rules or precedence to work out the logic behind an argument.
- ◆ *Creativity:* Identifying numerous, varied, and unique solutions to generic problems.
- ◆ *Spatial ability:* Imagining how shapes can rotate in three dimensional space.
- ◆ *Dexterity:* Working quickly or with fine precision on manual tasks.
- ◆ *Sensory ability:* Discriminating sounds, colors, or other stimuli involving a person's five senses.

Along with the generic ability tests discussed above, practitioners have at their disposal a treasure trove of knowledge- and skill-based tests. As mentioned earlier, tests of knowledge and skill are more directly related than ability tests to the specific training a person has received in preparation for a job. Knowledge tests could investigate whether individuals are aware of prominent theories in the field or laws specific to their practices. For example, the multiple-choice test about road rules endured by learner drivers is an example of a knowledge test.

In contrast, the practical component of the licensing process where applicants are observed on the road by an examiner is an example of a skills test. Tests of skill question how well you put your knowledge into action. In the workplace, skill testing often includes clerical skills or the use of technology (for example, working with a specific computer package).

Irrespective of whether the test is knowledge-, skill-, or ability-based, it has to pass certain criteria to be considered a reliable and valid form of assessment. The output of the test has to be quantifiable, such that a person's test score can be compared to those of others who previously completed the test. The comparison group (often called the *norm group*, due to its normal distribution) determines how well the individual performed relative to his or her peers. As an alternative, candidate scores can be compared to performance metrics to determine what a "good" score looks like (termed *criterion referenced*); however, norm referencing is much more common across test providers.

Beyond how the test was built and selected for use, it should be administered and scored in a consistent fashion. Testing conditions, instructions and practice questions, the time given to candidates, and the process for scoring should be clearly defined and applied equally to all candidates undergoing assessment. This requires that all assessors be trained in the test content and the process of administering it to candidates.

The last two decades have seen a dramatic change in how tests are administered to candidates. Online technology has allowed tests to be administered to candidates anywhere in the world. Results are processed in seconds, and hiring managers can begin making their hiring choices within minutes of test completion. Each test is unique, with questions randomly chosen from a large database. In some cases, computer-adapted technology is used to match questions to how well the candidate is performing on the test as a way of shortening the total testing time.

Such improvements do not come without costs. Online testing is often performed unsupervised and, as a result, candidates may believe that there are few risks to having a friend or relative substitute for them. Recent research undertaken in the UK discovered that as many as 10 percent of candidates would cheat on an ability test if they thought they could get away with it. Beyond issues of dishonesty, the reach of online testing crosses national borders and may challenge legal or cultural beliefs about their proper use. Some practitioners have even considered prescreening candidates, putting test results on a system that can be accessed by employers (similar to how standardized test scores are used by universities to screen applicants). Such practices raise ethical questions about who owns the data, whether it is appropriate for general use, and how long the test results are valid for.

When done right, tests of knowledge, skills, and ability provide objective information that can be used by employers to validate a candidate's capability to do a job. The real question is whether the tests do more than simply validate what has already been claimed on a candidate's résumé. From my perspective, the ease of administering tests has led to an inflation in the number of assessments a candidate is required to complete. If a candidate applies for multiple positions, the time and effort given to assessment is substantial, especially in combination with interviews. Whether employers should trust universities, previous employers, and professional bodies to provide and accredit knowledge and skills to avoid further testing is up for debate.

# Work Simulations

If we return to our scenario of buying a house, work simulations would not really involve the home inspector at all. Instead, work simulations would be analogous to the interested buyers moving in and living in the house for a short time before they committed to the purchase. The buyers could experience for themselves how long the hot water lasts, whether the neighborhood feels safe at 2 a.m., and whether their commute to the office really is that much better on the north side of town. If you had the option to buy the apartments you have rented, I imagine that the shortlist would be very short indeed.

In the workplace, simulations allow both the candidate and hiring manager to evaluate whether the job fit is a good one. When simulations are a strong representation of the types of responsibilities or behaviors expected on the job, the candidate can gain insight about whether he or she would like taking on the role, whereas the candidate's observable performance can provide an indication to the employer about his or her capability.

In this section, I will provide a brief tour of workplace simulations, which can vary greatly in how they are constructed and administered. I will then share with you how the world of simulation is changing through both advanced forms of technology and a desire by companies to project a consistent employer brand. I end this section with a critique of the technique, arguing that we have a long way to go to ensure all employers are applying a reliable and valid form of assessment in their simulations.

## THE DREADED ASSESSMENT CENTER

Work simulations are rarely experienced in isolation. They are typically bundled into half-day or full-day packages that exhaust and challenge even the most capable candidates. Alongside simulations, candidates may endure ability tests, psychometrics, and interviews, all wrapped up in the term *assessment center.*

The origins of assessment centers can be traced back to the 1930s, when occupational psychologists used a series of simulations to evaluate the capability of military officers in both Germany and Great Britain. After World War II, the British Civil Service continued the practice in their selection for managerial roles. The term "assessment center" was coined in the 1950s and refers to an actual building on the AT&T campus where recruiters brought applicants to undergo workplace simulations. The technique steadily grew in popularity and, by 1989, Shackleton and Newell estimated that 60 percent of companies were using workplace simulations.

There are a wide range of simulation types. They can be broken into five general categories based on what the candidate is asked to do:

- ◆ **Role plays:** Candidates are asked to take on a role and interact with an actor to resolve some burning issue. Typical role plays can involve negotiating with a customer, coaching a direct report, or reporting business results to their manager. A variation on the role play is called a "fact-find," where candidates attempt to extract information from the actor.

- ◆ **Presentations:** After considering business-relevant information, candidates are asked to present a strategy that is evaluated by an assessor. Typical presentations look at the launch of a new product, mergers between companies, or balancing the needs of competing business divisions.

- ◆ **In-trays:** Candidates are presented with an "in-tray" of e-mails, memos, requests, letters, advertisements, or press clippings and asked to find issues that have to be addressed, prioritize them by urgency and importance, and make decisions about what next steps are required.

- ◆ **Group exercise:** Working in a group of four to six, candidates talk through and seek a resolution to a business issue. The group is asked not to assign an official chairperson, allowing group members to interact with minimal constraint. In an "assigned role" variation of the group exercise, each candidate is provided with a unique piece of information that forces everyone to participate. Another variant on the group exercise pits groups of candidates against each other in a market environment, as a form of business game.

- ◆ **Written exercise:** Candidates are asked to write a response or evaluate a business topic. The information presented can be abrasive, as a means of assessing how tactful and professional candidates are in their responses.

In putting together an assessment center, a matrix is created that identifies which exercises are included in the design and the targeted criteria. Although designs can vary, behavioral competencies are typically used as the anchor to judge candidate performance. For example, a presentation exercise attempts to measure a candidate's strategic thinking and commercial acumen, whereas a role play may focus on the candidate's persuasiveness and comfort in dealing with conflict. The general rule of thumb promoted by practitioners is to limit the number of competencies assessed by any given exercise to two or three and to ensure that each competency can be easily observed by assessors.

Once the design matrix has been drafted (Figure 3.7), a timetable can be drawn up that is used by candidates, assessors, and actors throughout the center. When considering that the average full-day assessment center would typically involve six candidates, three assessors, three actors, and a test administrator across four exercises, the timetable is a miracle of planning (Figure 3.8). There is a sense of accomplishment every time a practitioner successfully manages to get everyone in the right place at the right time. The additional logistics of candidate and assessor communications, printing materials, and online tool completion beforehand leads me to recommend that inexperienced practitioners seek advice before attempting to run an assessment program on their own.

Depending on the simulation chosen, the role and number of assessors can vary. When using presentations, assessors are typically the ones being presented to. For in-trays and written exercises, assessors normally read and score candidate responses after the experience. Assessors observe the interaction between actors and candidates during role plays, whereas in group exercises assessors

| | Role Play | Presentation | Ability Test | Interview |
|---|---|---|---|---|
| Competency 1 | ✓ | | | ✓ |
| Competency 2 | | ✓ | ✓ | |
| Competency 3 | ✓ | | | ✓ |
| Competency 4 | | ✓ | | ✓ |

FIGURE 3.7  Simple Example of an Assessment Matrix

| | Candidate 1 | Candidate 2 | Candidate 3 | Candidate 4 | Candidate 5 | Candidate 6 |
|---|---|---|---|---|---|---|
| 9.00–10.15 | Group Exercise<br>Room 1, A1 = C1 + C4 : A2 = C2 + C5 : A3 = C3 + C6 | | | | | |
| 10.15–10.30 | Break<br>Reception Area | | | | | |
| 10.30–11.30 | Preparation Time<br>Room 1 | | | Role Play<br>Room 2, A3 | Role Play<br>Room 3, A1 | Role Play<br>Room 4, A2 |
| 11.30–12.00 | Presentation<br>Room 2, A2 | Presentation<br>Room 3, A3 | Presentation<br>Room 4, A1 | Lunch<br>Room 1 | | |
| 12.00–12.30 | Lunch<br>Room 1 | | | Ability Test<br>Room 4 | | |
| 12.30–13.30 | Role Play<br>Room 2, A3 | Role Play<br>Room 3, A1 | Role Play<br>Room 4, A2 | Preparation Time<br>Room 1 | | |
| 13.30–14.00 | Ability Test<br>Room 1 | | | Presentation<br>Room 2, A2 | Presentation<br>Room 3, A3 | Presentation<br>Room 4, A1 |

FIGURE 3.8 Simple Example of an Assessment Center Timetable

observe two of the candidates at the same time. Each exercise must be carefully studied and multiple responses observed to gage what a good response looks like. When observing live exercises, assessors must observe and record the content accurately and without bias, saving all evaluation until later.

Just like other forms of assessment, the reliability and validity of workplace simulations suffer when instructions or the time permitted to candidates is inconsistent. Moreover, structured actor briefings and rating forms both contribute to the methodology's effectiveness.

### TRENDS IN SIMULATION

In the discussion about assessment centers, an assumption exists that workplace simulations will be presented in a paper-and-pencil format. The new world of assessment has brought the technique online, where candidates experience simulations in their own time and at a location of their choosing. The simplest form of online simulations present scenarios in a written format, asking candidates to choose how they would resolve the problem by using multiple-choice options. Such tools provide no real advantage to paper-based alternatives and, in some cases, have less influence on candidate perceptions about the job and leave assessors with limited insight on capability.

The latest versions of online simulations take full advantage of computer technology by using video, animation, or avatars to create a more realistic simulation of human interaction. Currently on the market are standardized assessments for front-line managers, clerical workers, call-center employees, and retailers. The trick behind the construction of these new tools is in the scripting; each question is independent and does not conflict with future decisions made by the candidate.

Whether traditional or online, organizations have increasingly been interested in developing simulations that look and feel like the real workplace, as way of promoting a strong and consistent employer brand image. Assessment centers with exercises that present information with a likeness to the job, strung together with consistent content, are sometimes referred to as *day-in-the-life* experiences. Online simulations that pay particular attention to look, feel, and realistic content are categorized into two basic types, depending on how information is used. *Situational judgment tests* use candidate performance on the simulation for screening or selection, whereas *realistic job previews* provide an experience purely for candidates to gain a preview of job responsibilities.

I will now focus on how workplace simulations (online and traditional) are constructed, administered, and scored, so that you can evaluate for yourself their potential benefits and drawbacks for your organization. On the surface, tailored workplace simulations provide more benefit to hiring managers and candidates than their generic alternatives. Information is gleaned on a candidate's capability to perform job responsibilities, while candidates can get a feel for the job and organization, at times self-selecting themselves out of the process if they think the fit is poor.

However, this is only half the story. Generic workplace simulations often have an increased level of validation that is not available for tailored versions. Job analysis with incumbents and managers is the foundation from which tailored simulations are made. Great skill is required to translate these interviews into an exercise that can be completed equally by internal and external candidates, especially when the simulation is used for multiple roles. Mistakes can also be made in translating workplace responsibilities to observable tasks, so that clear exercise ratings can be given. Drafts of tailored simulations are often validated only by interviews with subject-matter experts, rather than through a thorough study of content, construct, and criterion validity.

Although some generic simulations may be more robust in their construction, they, too, can be problematic. Deciding on the type of roles and level an exercise applies to is central to the process when it's used for hiring or promotion. Even with a flawless design, candidates are placed in an artificial environment when they go to an assessment center and, to a lesser extent, this is true of an online simulation. The pressures brought on by assessment, where candidates try to guess the "right" response, are forced to interact with each other, and are observed by an army of unfamiliar people can have a negative impact on performance.

Recent criticism argues that scores reflect candidates' ability to identify the target competency (termed *ability to identify criteria)* and adjust their behavior accordingly, rather than assessing their underlying capability. For example, strong candidates in a group exercise may have figured out that the exercise assesses teamwork and, therefore, done their best to interact equally with everyone seated at the table. To counteract the artificial nature of simulations, some practitioners conduct a post-exercise interview, taking into account how an individual approached the exercise into the final evaluation. These interviews can tease out the difference between conscious strategies (adjusting behavior or omitting information) from a lack of understanding of the scenario.

Scoring of workplace simulations can also be problematic. Inter-rater reliability plays a major part in whether findings from simulations can be relied on when making personnel decisions. Unlike online simulations (which are still in the minority), traditional simulations require an observer to determine how well a candidate has performed. Structured rating forms and assessor training with practical examples only go so far in adding objectivity and robustness to the process. Fundamentally, each response to a simulation is unique, which is both the power and the drawback of simulations. Unless the hiring manager observes all candidates undergoing the same simulation and weighs different approaches and each candidate's fit to the job, then bias will creep into the process.

In the last few years, questions have been raised over exactly what can and should be measured by workplace simulations. As already mentioned, the default position is to use behavioral competencies. Each exercise is assumed to be valid for measuring a limited number (usually two or three) of competencies. For example, an in-tray could measure organizing, decision making, and delivering on customer needs. Meta-analyses on assessment centers have found that scoring competencies across exercises is not as effective as providing a score for each exercise as a whole. For example, a score for an in-tray as a whole could be used to judge how effectively candidates are able to manage a similar workload, with an equal amount of complexity, in the real world. By shifting scoring methodology from competency to exercise, a clearer link can be made to the workplace (if the choice of exercise is right) and, more interestingly, judgments can be made about what a good response would be based on how similar scenarios play out in the real world.

On the whole, workplace simulations may be tapping issues of capability that would otherwise not be accomplished by interviews or tests of knowledge, skills, and ability. A "try before you buy" approach is compelling, especially when little is known about a candidate or the candidate is external to the company. Yet, I have encountered more than my fair share of poorly executed business simulations. Back-of-the-envelope exercises are continually being thrown at candidates. I can recall one instance when I was asked to interview another candidate for the same job I had applied for as a form of role play. This placed me in an ethical dilemma that no candidate should experience. If I went too hard on my competition, he or she might do the same to me when it was his or her turn. Going soft was equally bad, as I would fail to demonstrate the skills the company wanted to recruit. Needless to say, I didn't get the job and am thankful for that outcome; we would have been a horrible match.

## Where to from Here?

Before I weigh the benefits and potential problems with current-day practices for assessing capability, I want to look at two issues that may complicate matters. The first is whether hiring managers are measuring candidates against current needs or future potential. This is particularly important for internal candidates who either willingly or unwillingly participate in programs to assess their generic potential for promotion. Such assessments are high risk for candidates, as their assessment results may bear little relation to their performance on the job. Moreover, they may be exposed to new managers for whom they have not worked. If they perform badly, candidates are likely branded as having little potential and discouraged from any future competitions. Opportunities for development may also pass them by.

Second, assessment data can be used out of context once gathered. I have witnessed clients attempting to apply assessment data to other personnel decisions with little relation to the original event. Out of context, assessment data is meaningless, as it was captured in relation to a specific job, with a unique set of job criteria, and against a group of other candidates. Even if the data is to be used for a future competition involving the same job, there is a life expectancy attached to any assessment. Candidates gain skills and experience that can improve their ability to perform job duties, whereas personal circumstances change that affect motivation. Without trained practitioners, such factors can be missed and the data wrongfully interpreted.

Taking these two issues into account, it is up to practitioners to determine for themselves not only which tools have the right makeup to tap candidate capabilities that will predict future success, but also the process for collecting and using this information. In this chapter, I presented a wide range of tools for assessing capability, ranging from interviews and tests of knowledge, skills, and abilities to workplace simulations. I have given statistics about their predictability, have identified how they are typically misused in the workplace, and provided tips about how the techniques could be improved.

When evaluating whether your own organization is using assessments appropriately (or if you are new to assessment, which ones you should adopt), I would encourage you to ask whether the assessments are differentiating on the characteristics that truly matter for the job and organization. Do they take a whole person approach, rather than focusing too narrowly on only one defining characteristic? Are the techniques applied in a reliable fashion, where every candidate is given an equal chance to succeed?

From my experience, the answer to these questions is not straightforward. Things become even more complicated when assessments are used across jobs and organizational levels. Poor job analysis can lead to ill-constructed assessments that were not implemented in a fair or objective manner. I have witnessed the misuse of assessment data and the unfortunate negative branding of employees following failure in assessment centers. Yet when capability assessments are done right, the information gleaned can be invaluable and save a company from making a poor hiring or promotion decision. Assessments provide a safety net for understanding a candidate's likelihood for success when past performance is unknown and, for this reason, I believe the positives outweigh the negatives.

# Chapter 4

## Psychometric Assessment

Capability only tells half the story when it comes to predicting employee performance. Candidates may hold a vast array of knowledge, skills, and experience, but whether they deploy their capability for the benefit of the company is often described as a person's *motivation*. Pinder (1998) provides a basic definition of motivation as the "Set of energetic forces that originate both within as well as beyond an individual's being, to initiate work-related behavior and to determine its form, direction, intensity, and duration." Motivation is so central to the relationship between capability and performance that most practitioners give it equal footing in the following equation:

$$Performance = Capability \times Motivation$$

Employee motivation challenges the organizational perspective of capability, where experience and skills are demanded by the job. Motivation cannot be checked off a list, but instead is dynamic, ebbing and flowing in concert with the employee-employer relationship. What once motivated them as new hires may hold little importance for older and more established employees, due to the fulfillment of needs or a decrease in their relevance for personal satisfaction and well-being. How and why these changes occur rests partially in the employees' life experiences, but also with societal and economic pressures that lie outside of their control.

This does not mean that motivation should be ignored. Rather, practitioners have consistently pinpointed motivation as the key driver for employee engagement. By understanding what motivates employees at various times in their lives and adapting the workplace environment accordingly, employers can improve the employment relationship and, through it, both employee engagement and job performance. As a result, focus shifts from organizational demands of capability to valuing the interaction between staff and the workplace.

This chapter focuses on how motivation is understood and acted upon by employers. I will discuss three major forms of motivation, based on the fulfillment of needs, traits, or values. Over the past century, occupational psychologists have created a vast array of techniques for gathering information about candidates that, when compared to others, can be used to predict how well they are likely to fit a new workplace. An underlying assumption is that a stronger alignment between an individual's motivational profile and the workplace will lead to stronger engagement and performance.

This is all fine in principle. But, in practice, there is potential for psychometric assessments to misrepresent candidates early in the employment relationship, sabotaging their bids for a job or a promotion. Assumptions can be made that a person's motivational profile reflects his or her *capability* to perform a task, rather than *willingness* to consistently engage in the work. This is compounded with a variety of dubious psychometrics on the market that lack sufficient reliability or validity. At a more fundamental level, psychometric assessment is seldom used to adjust the workplace to meet an individual's needs. Instead, assessments are used to remove individuals who will not fully conform to the workplace environment, which makes for a very one-sided approach to the employment relationship.

There is hope on the horizon, as advanced psychometric techniques may offer a means of objectively assessing person-environment fit. Whether or not these new techniques convince employers to rebalance the way they use psychometrics is too early to call.

## But First, an Experiment

Below are three personality descriptions of a famous figure from the 20th century. Only one is based on a psychological model of personality with a well-researched form of measurement. Can you guess which passage has a psychological basis and who the famous person is?

## PASSAGE 1

You have a cautious and conservative approach, with a good head for business. You are pleasant to be around and have many affectionate relationships. Naturally shy and introverted, you seldom lose your temper and work hard to avoid conflict. When conflict arises, you approach it calmly and considerately, hardly ever raising your voice or becoming visibly annoyed. It is not unusual for you to have a flood of ideas and, being guided by this inspiration, you venture into unknown territory by starting new activities. Your ideas are based on reality and focused on practicality. Others would describe you as a pioneer and praise you for your innovations. The challenge is in keeping your energy up, as you tend to get bored easily and to seek out opportunities elsewhere before finishing all your commitments.

## PASSAGE 2

You are characterized by a combination of intelligence and creative insight. It might be difficult to make friends easily at first, but once established, your relationships are lasting. You invest considerably into your personal relationships, expressing a great degree of compassion and devotion to others, although you can find it difficult to make tough decisions, especially when they have the potential to harm others. You have a need to express yourself artistically and, due to your creatively, may find it difficult dealing with practical issues, such as managing finances. You have an ability to see future trends and guide others toward a vision about what the world could be like. However, you tend to be introverted and must make an effort to ensure your voice is heard.

## PASSAGE 3

You are an independent problem solver who excels at providing a detached, concise analysis of an idea. You ask difficult questions, challenging others and yourself to find new logical approaches. You work well independently, especially on problems with solutions that run counter to prevailing wisdom. You approach almost everything with skepticism and enjoy forming your own opinions of the world around you. You see possibilities and connections beyond the present and obvious, finding it difficult to take on routine tasks or deal with practicalities. You are usually quiet and reserved, although you can be talkative in areas where you are most knowledgeable. When stressed, you might erupt outwardly in inappropriate displays of emotion, which have the potential to unnerve others.

Have you spotted the psychologically sound personality description? Can you hazard a guess as to who the famous person is?

The first and second passages capture a description of personality purely based on our famous person's birthday. The first is a description of an Earth Rabbit from the Chinese Zodiac, associated with the year 1879. The second passage describes the personality characteristics of someone who is born on the fourteenth of March, falling within the astrological sign of Pisces. The third passage provides a psychological description of personality, based on an INTP personality type from the Myers Briggs Type Indicator (MBTI), which has routinely been associated with Albert Einstein.

If you look back at these three descriptions, the language used is eerily similar, and even the content has a great deal of overlap. If Einstein were alive today, it would be interesting to know what he would make of this. Would he discount the exercise fully, or would he recognize glimmers of truth in the descriptions? If he was like the rest of us, he might see them as fairly accurate reflections of his personality. This effect was first recognized by Forer in 1948 and fondly referred to since as the "Barnum effect," so termed from P.T. Barnum's remark that "we've got something for everyone."

The Barnum effect describes a tendency for individuals to ascribe high accuracy ratings to descriptions of their personalities that, although the descriptions appear tailored to them, are, in fact, vague and generic. The effect is strongest when the subject is invested in receiving feedback, believes in the authority of the evaluator, and is provided with a long list of positive traits to ponder.

This experiment illustrates that personality language is evocative and powerful, setting our expectations of what someone would be like and guiding our perceptions in a self-fulfilling way. Personality provides a shorthand for understanding the drives and motives of others. Yet, how certain can we be that the tools we are relying on are valid and reliable? Below, we will explore the basis for some common models of personality, as well as the psychometrics used in their measurement. As you are reading through the following sections, I encourage you to reflect on this experiment and your ability (or inability) to discern among the three descriptions.

# Employee Needs

We have all heard the phrase "the carrot or the stick" when motivation is discussed. These approaches share the common view that other people have the power to change your personal behavior. This is the most straightforward interpretation of motivation, with the theories that underlie it (referred to as *need* theories) aimed at identifying what employees desire the most and how managers can fulfill those desires. Sometimes, it is about physically providing employees with tangible rewards as a form of *extrinsic* motivation. Other times, it is about leaving employees alone to do what they like best, often referred to as *intrinsic* motivation.

When desires go unfilled, motivation wanes and can sometimes lead to employees leaving the company. Some motivators take priority in this respect. RedBalloon recently polled 3,000 employees in Australia and New Zealand, discovering that 52 percent of employees believe that a lack of recognition by their managers would encourage them to quit their jobs. This statistic is more frightening when considering that 62 percent of respondents described their managers' level of praise as insufficient, with 20 percent of employees receiving no praise whatsoever. According to Talent Drain (2008), other important motivators that lead to turnover include a lack of promotion, lack of development opportunities, and a poor relationship with the immediate manager.

One of the oldest need theories of motivation attempts to sort out what motivators are necessary for an individual's well-being. Maslow's Hierarchy of Needs, originally developed in 1943, proposes that the achievement of lower level needs provides the freedom to seek out higher level needs. At the lowest level in the hierarchy, individuals are thought to seek ways of satisfying deficiencies in *physiological* needs, satisfied through the provision of financial reward. The second level in the hierarchy involves *safety* through the creation of stability and predictability, which could be represented by a permanent offer of employment. The third level is *love,* with the establishment of affectionate relations with others, such as with work colleagues. The fourth level involves *esteem*, where an individual seeks respect and achievement. This could occur through accomplishing difficult work objectives or being recognized for exceptional performance. The final level is *actualization*, characterized by individuals fulfilling their full potential. Employees who feel that they have found the perfect vocation and who are engrossed in its pursuits may be described as attaining this level in the hierarchy.

A second and equally influential model is provided by Herzberg (1968), who suggested two distinct forms of motivators. *Hygiene* factors, similar to the lower levels in Maslow's hierarchy, have the potential to demotivate employees if not provided for, but do little to encourage employees to work harder. The provision of pleasant work conditions, stable pay, supportive supervision, and the opportunity for social interaction are thought to create an environment that allows employees to fulfill basic job requirements. To encourage employees to work harder, Herzberg suggested that organizations provide motivators such as *personal responsibility, challenging work*, and *opportunities for professional growth*.

As a modern example of a need theory, Warr questions whether you could ever have too much of a good thing, in his "vitamin model" of motivation. Individuals experiencing a high level of fulfillment are expected to demonstrate affective well-being, competence to perform job requirements, aspiration to grow in their vocation, autonomy in how they go about their work, and social integration with peers. Warr identified a set of primary motivators that are thought to follow a U-shaped relationship with motivation, whereby both low and excessive levels are thought to hinder an employee's mental health. These include:

- ♦ Opportunity for control,
- ♦ Opportunity for skill use,
- ♦ Externally generated goals,
- ♦ Variety,
- ♦ Environmental clarity, and
- ♦ Opportunity for interpersonal contact.

Like beta carotene in carrots that can turn you orange when you eat too many, some motivators can damage the employment relationship. The remaining job features, enough money, physical security, and a valued social position, are considered universally good for mental health, as are the three organizational features of having a supportive supervisor, career outlook, and equity. Like Vitamin C, there appears to be no limit to how much you can have of these motivators.

Common across the three models is the identification of employee needs that can be satisfied by the workplace. Depending on the dimension, fulfillment of needs is thought to result in motivation that itself creates higher job performance. However, what these models fail to mention is whether denying motivators that were once provided, as a form of punishment, can have an equal effect on performance. The models as they stand are more about the carrot than the stick.

There is a subtle, yet important difference between the models. Both Maslow and Herzberg share a universal approach to motivation, whereby all individuals value lower level motivators equally. This is not inherent to Warr's model or the way that motivation is applied in the modern workplace. Most psychometrics today ask participants either directly or indirectly about what motivates them in the workplace. Comparing their answers against those of other workers, a profile is built of an individual's top and bottom motivators.

These motivators are thought to help explain what attracts people to an organization, whether they will consistently perform in their jobs, and whether they will contribute through good organizational citizenship behavior. If used early in the employment relationship or during times of transition, such information about an employee can be used to monitor how things are going from the employee's perspective, complementing the employer's emphasis on performance.

Yet, there are many words of caution here. When motivators are explicitly discussed and actions agreed on, expectations are set with an employee. When expectations are left unfulfilled due to over-promising or through the manager's ignorance about what could be accomplished, greater damage may result than if the topic was never raised in the first place. The other risk is that employees may feel uncomfortable discussing their personal preferences openly, especially if they were just hired. In such cases, managers may rely heavily on psychometrics, which may or may not be a good reflection of what the employee really wants. The generic vocabulary used by the psychometric may confuse matters further if the content is not confirmed with the employee.

Research on need-based motivation often conflicts with common practice in the private sector. A series of fascinating studies have recently investigated the disparity between what senior leaders think motivates staff and the reality as experienced by workers. Contrary to recommendations by consultants, pay-for-performance fails to deliver anything beyond the completion of basic jobs. Performance-related pay for complex or cognitively demanding jobs actually detracts from performance, leading to disruptive behaviors and priorities. Money is important, but only to a point and, in my experience, it becomes an issue among staff when there are other grievances. Grumbling about pay is often a symptom of underlying ills plaguing the employment relationship, such as a lack of progression and development opportunities, or broken promises.

The best recommendation is to take money and other basic needs off the table (fulfill the hygiene factors). From there, provide opportunities for employees to build competence and work under their own direction, making it apparent how their work contributes to the greater good (themes aligned to Deci and Ryan's Self-Determination Theory). Then, after having a thorough understanding of each employee, begin tailoring the employment relationship based on individual needs. In some cases, fulfillment involves merely standing out of the way and letting employees do what they love most. This is the crossover point with the next type of motivation, personality traits.

## Personality Traits

Unlike need theories that focus on satisfaction brought on by a positive workplace, *personality* relates to our internal drives that, when suppressed, can lead to anxiety or other negative emotions. Personality traits include such divergent themes as how social someone is, whether he or she feels comfortable leaving tasks unfulfilled, or whether he or she is comfortable sharing emotions. Personality traits lead to consistency in employee behavior over time and across situations and, thus, are of interest to occupational psychologists. Debate rages about the most appropriate model for use in occupational settings, whether testing of personality leads to typecasting, and whether there are any universally helpful personality dimensions that drive performance or employee satisfaction.

The debate is warranted, as the use of personality in occupational settings has been built on shaky foundations. Early models of personality focused on an individual's physical characteristics to determine what type of personality he or she had. For example, Sheldon in the 1940s identified three primary temperaments that were linked to body shape. *Mesomorphs* have a muscular physique and, therefore, were thought prone to aggression and risk taking. *Endomorphs* are short and plump in stature, meaning that they were extraverted and fun-loving. Last, *Ectomorphs* are skinny and were characterized as being shy and inhibited.

Underlying such models is an assumption that personality type can be easily recognized. Other debunked models focus on anything from star signs (astrology) to penmanship (graphology), and the bumps on your head (phrenology) to identify and categorize personality (Figures 4.1 and 4.2).

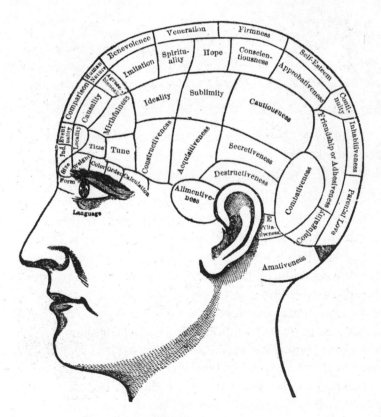

FIGURE **4.1**  Image of Phrenological Organs

*Source:* Wellcome Library, London, Phrenological Organs, 1887. Used with permission.

**FIGURE 4.2**   Image of a Servants' Employment Agency Where Heads Are Examined to Determine Suitability

*Source:* Wellcome Library, London. Used by permission.

Then there are those techniques that linger on, despite issues of interpretation and subjectivity. Projective techniques of personality present individuals with ambiguous shapes, pictures, or words (the most well known is the Rorschach test). Practitioners interpret the individual's associations, pinpointing personality type (Figure 4.3). A second technique is to focus on biodata, whereby a person's experiences and interests are thought indicative of specific personality types. I have seen a variety of recruiters use résumés in this way; however, without an independent method for validating why someone chose those experiences (or even whether he had a choice), any conclusions about personality rest on dubious ground.

By far the most widely accepted way of assessing personality is by questionnaire. The technique is surprisingly old, arising out of the

FIGURE **4.3**  Image of a Sample Inkblot Used in Projective Techniques
*Source:* Public domain.

"Personal Data Sheet" used for assessing neurotic behavior among soldiers in World War I. Early questionnaires relied on the observation of psychologists, but then evolved into self-report versions utilizing an inventory of items (for example, the Bernreuter Personality Inventory for Neurotic Tendency, Self-Sufficiency, Introversion, and Dominance).

The most widely used questionnaire is the Minnesota Multiphasic Personality Inventory, which when developed in the 1940s, used mental patients to determine item selection. The California Personality Inventory was developed a decade later, concentrating on social and intellectual effectiveness. Both questionnaires focus on mental health and, therefore, are not typically used by practitioners working in occupational settings.

Although such clinical tools sit at the far end of personality tools in their relevance to the workplace, they have stirred debate among practitioners about how far into someone's personal life they should look. On one side, workplace behavior is argued as inseparable from what is going on in someone's personal life. Significant events, financial or familial pressures, or the individual's background, it is argued, spill into the workplace. By exploring these drives, some practitioners claim greater accuracy in predicting the outcomes of recruitment decisions or development initiatives.

On the other side of the debate, personality can be considered as context-dependent. Somebody's preferences or typical way of behaving at work is not necessarily the same as he or she behaves in family or social circles. High amounts of sociability, organization, or openness to new experiences can mean different things if talking about going out this weekend or taking on a new work assignment.

The ramification of this debate is that many personality tools have been developed across the home/work continuum. Tools like the Occupational Personality Questionnaire (OPQ) sits firmly on the "work in isolation" end. Developed in the 1980s, the OPQ was designed specifically for the workplace, avoiding clinical constructs and adopting language that could be easily used by the human resources community. The resulting model identifies thirty-two dimensions that fall into the three broad categories of Relationships with People, Thinking Style, and Feelings and Emotion.

Sitting within the integrated personality perspective, the Myers Briggs Type Indicator (MBTI) does not differentiate between home or work life. The tool was first developed in the 1940s as a means of making Carl Jung's model of personality accessible to a wider audience. The resulting model is based on dichotomies (Extraversion vs. Introversion, Intuition vs. Sensing, Thinking vs. Feeling, and Judgment vs. Perception), whereby an individual's personality type (e.g., ENTP) is thought to influence behavior within both social and work relationships.

The OPQ and MBTI differ in two other fundamental ways that also apply broadly to other psychometrics frequently used by practitioners. First, the OPQ and MBTI are, respectively, *trait-* and *type-based* tools. With *trait-based* tools, the quantity of a given dimension is measured, compared against a norm group of a similar demographic, and assessed for fit against an ideal profile. With a *type-based* tool, a number of dimensions are combined to define an individual's personality. Individuals are sorted into distinctive categories without regard for the amount of a given personality trait someone has, as a means of drawing comparisons between individuals and their unique psychological drives.

Second, the tools differ in their development, being either empirically (OPQ) (see Figure 4.4) or theoretically (MBTI) founded.

| RELATIONSHIPS WITH PEOPLE | | 1 | 2 | 3 | 4 | 5 | 6 | 7 | 8 | 9 | 10 | | |
|---|---|---|---|---|---|---|---|---|---|---|---|---|---|
| | | | | | | **INFLUENCE** | | | | | | | |
| 9 | rarely pressures others to change their views, dislikes selling, less comfortable using negotiation | | | | | | | | | Persuasive | | enjoys selling, comfortable using negotiation, likes to change other people's view | |
| 5 | happy to let others take charge, dislikes telling people what to do, unlikely to take the lead | | | | | Controlling | | | | | | likes to be in charge, takes the lead, tells others what to do, takes control | |
| 1 | holds back from criticizing others, may not express own views, unprepared to put forward own opinions | | Outspoken | | | | | | | | | freely expresses opinions, makes disagreement clear, prepared to criticize others | |
| 3 | accepts majority decision, prepared to follow the consensus | | | Independent Minded | | | | | | | | prefers to follow own approach, prepared to disregard majority decisions | |
| | | | | | | **SOCIABILITY** | | | | | | | |
| 5 | quiet and reserved in groups, dislikes being center of attention | | | | | Outgoing | | | | | | lively and animated in groups, talkative, enjoys attention | |
| 7 | comfortable spending time away from people, values time spent alone, seldom misses the company of others | | | | | | | Affiliative | | | | enjoys others' company, likes to be around people, can miss the company of others | |
| 8 | feels more comfortable in less formal situations, can feel awkward when first meeting people | | | | | Socially Confident | | | | | | feels comfortable when first meeting people, at ease in formal situations | |
| | | | | | | **EMPATHY** | | | | | | | |
| 5 | makes strengths and achievements known, talks about personal success | | | | | Modest | | | | | | dislikes discussing achievements, keeps quiet about personal success | |
| 2 | prepared to make decisions without consultation, prefers to make decisions alone | | Democratic | | | | | | | | | consults widely, involves others in decision making, less likely to make decisions alone | |
| 6 | selective with sympathy and support, remains detached from others' personal problems | | | | | | Caring | | | | | sympathetic and considerate towards others, helpful and supportive, gets involved in others' problems | |

FIGURE 4.4  Example of Dimensions from a Personality Profile

*Source:* SHL, Occupational Personality Questionnaire (OPQ), courtesy of CEB. © SHL, a part of CEB. All rights reserved. Used with permission.

Empirical tools are built ground up, whereby personality dimensions and categories are identified through individual responses to questionnaire items. Theoretical tools are built top down, with a specific model of personality articulated into questionnaire items that are later validated with a group of respondents. Of all the models, the Five Factor Model of Personality (Big Five) is the most substantiated by the research. The factors of Openness, Conscientiousness, Extraversion, Agreeableness, and Neuroticism are used as a standard to assess the inclusiveness of a variety of psychometrics and incorporated explicitly in the construction of Cattell's 16PF tool.

These differences aside, psychometrics are incredibly powerful in changing how people think about themselves and others. There is a mystique about personality that is not so different from having a palm read or hearing about the future from a psychic. Psychometrics tell a story about an individual, identifying his or her likes and dislikes, how these compare to those of others, and the types of behavior that are likely to result. They provide the "why" behind how someone acts in the workplace, uncovering motivations that would otherwise be hidden from view.

Yet, there are three problems with this picture. First, personality tools are not equal in their construction or application. How close they tap into workplace preferences (whether home and work life are integrated), whether they are aligned to features of the job (trait instead of type tools), or based on firm theoretical and empirical foundations—all affect how reliable and valid the tools are for use in occupational settings. When used for self-awareness in development, these issues do not matter so much, as the psychometrics are simply providing a mirror for participants to learn more about themselves, their co-workers, and the workplace. If used in selection decisions, a lack of psychometric reliability and validity opens the door to assumption, a misrepresentation of candidate fit, and, ultimately, misguided decisions. If exposed, the poor use of psychometrics can justifiably be challenged in court.

Second, the application of psychometric testing is threatened by assessors taking questionnaire results too far. Practitioners and hiring managers alike can become intoxicated by the promise of enduring and inherent personality characteristics that predict success on the job. But this exaggerates the relationship between personality and behavior. Just because an individual prefers a certain way of acting does not mean that she will exhibit these preferences when at work. Employees make choices in the type of work they do, deciding between tasks where they gain the greatest satisfaction. Sometimes, employees take on work completely outside their preferences for the promise of later career advancement or because, in the end, the bills have to be paid and work cannot always be enjoyable.

Third, I would challenge that the use of psychometrics seldom serve the interests of employees. The information gleaned from personality measures are regularly used to evaluate whether a candidate fits the job. Yet, the converse is rarely considered. Employers often overlook whether the job offers the right mix of responsibilities or whether there is sufficient diversity in the motivations of the team. The imbalance of assessment, whereby both abilities and motivation are couched in the language of the hiring organization, leaves very little room for the employee's perspective in establishing a strong psychological contract. The demands of the organization outweigh the satisfaction of employee desires, which in my mind reduces the power that psychometrics play.

To defend against their improper use, organizations such as the British Psychological Society (BPS) have pushed for regulation. The UK system, which has been a pioneering force against bad practice, focuses on the competency of practitioners to make informed choices in the use of psychometrics. The system differentiates between the practitioners who use ability tests alone (Level 1) and those who can demonstrate the theoretical and practical issues involved in scoring, interpreting, and discussing personality measures (Level 2). Higher distinctions are also available for practitioners who use multiple personality tools (Level 3) and who demonstrate a great deal of knowledge (Chartered). Beyond the accreditation of practitioners, the BPS encourages organizations to draft a policy for the appropriate use of psychometrics that includes sections on the delegation of responsibilities, conditions for use, choice and interpretation of tools, equal opportunities, and confidentiality.

Despite the best of intentions, it is impossible for a self-regulating system to fully monitor the use of psychometrics. Test publishers require only a single accredited practitioner within each organization to buy their products, with the assumption that this individual will monitor all use and interpretation of candidate scores. Even if this does occur, an assumption is made that the accredited individual will make the right choices in applying the tools and will act consistently in interactions with hiring managers. For large or complex organizations using a wide range of psychometrics, this may be asking too much of any practitioner.

## Shared Values

Unlike employee needs or personality traits, which are rooted within an individual's preferences and are relatively stable across time, values are a social construct. They are formed through a person's interaction with others, with reflection about what they believe and agree with. The difference between goals and values is one of degree, with *values* representing overarching principles that apply across a wider range of social situations. Values lead to goal-directed behavior, with stronger values resulting in more direct, effortful, and sustained action. When *goals* are clearly articulated and monitored, they are powerful in shaping an employee's relationship with the employer. When their values are at odds, employees feel that they are fundamentally different from their workplace, leading to a break in their psychological contract, a loss of engagement, and potentially an exit from the organization.

The process of value formation through to goal-directed behavior is dependent on a chain of events. First, the employee has an experience that triggers recognition that some workplace characteristic is important. For example, if an employee feels that a colleague was wrongly passed over for promotion, the employee may begin valuing a merit-based workplace. Next, the employee will begin identifying with the value, looking for cues beyond the initial experience. Full integration of the value occurs when employees start acting in ways that are aligned to the value. In returning to the previous example, an employee could volunteer for a position on a selection panel for promotions.

Once established, the value affects the employees' self-concept, the behavioral norms adopted, and the goals they set for themselves and others. Pursuing a goal that is aligned to a value involves choice and commitment to use cognitive energy that could be used elsewhere. How much energy is spent depends on what has to be accomplished and the likelihood of outside resistance. A derivative of Vroom's Expectancy Theory, with a title that doesn't exactly roll off the tongue, is the Valence-Instrumentality-Expectancy Model, which holds that an individual's desire for the goal's outcome (valence), how strongly an action is related to the outcome (instrumentality), and a subjective prediction of the desired outcome occurring (expectancy) predicts the employee's commitment to his or her goal.

How the employee feels when seeking a goal is also thought to influence commitment, with positive emotion leading to greater goal attainment. In occupational settings, the concept of organizational justice is particularly influential for employee emotions. The ratio of inputs to outputs determines an employee's evaluation of organizational justice, resulting in either goal-relevant behavior if fairness and trust are perceived or tension when the imbalance is high. There are three different types of organizational justice: *distributive* (allocation of rewards), *procedural* (perceptions of the reward process), and *interactional* (perceptions about leader sincerity and objectiveness), each of which influences employee behavior, feelings of belonging, and self-esteem.

To summarize, values are formed through an employee's experience (good or bad), which can lead to goal-directed behavior either for or against the employer, depending on perceptions of what the employer values and level of organizational justice. Employees can either contribute to the employer (when aligned), work against the organization (when at odds), or simply drift away from lack of engagement.

Key to unpacking the relationship between value systems is the type of culture promoted within a given workplace. There is often a discrepancy between what leaders desire in their culture versus what employees experience on the ground, with the latter most useful for understanding how an individual's value system will affect his or her fit to the workplace. In general, organizations that promote self-acceptance, affiliation, and community-feeling experience greater employee satisfaction and alignment, whereas values centered on wealth and money are associated with poorer engagement. It is important to note that organizations do not have free reign in redefining their value systems, but are limited to constraints of local culture, which differ most on the dimensions of individualism, power distance, and short- or long-term time perspective.

Practitioners attempt to uncover whether a candidate's value system is aligned to that of the organization. Can the candidate adapt to a highly political environment, step up to internal competition, contribute ideas widely without being possessive, or make socially or environmentally conscious decisions? Such questions are routinely asked by hiring managers when choosing between candidates. Sometimes, values are incorporated into a behavioral competency model, which then becomes the basis for interview questions. Other companies prefer a less formal approach, by ushering candidates through multiple rounds of interviews, looking for a consensus as to whether the person will fit the office culture.

There is no doubt that alignment in values is of crucial importance to the psychological contract held between employees and their employers. Yet, the assessment of values typically falls short of identifying fit with any degree of certainty. Some organizations are lucky enough to truly have a shared cause, such as putting an end to poverty or becoming carbon neutral by 2020. Most organizations either haven't thought this through or need to find a cause that is related to their primary purpose (for example, sustainable logging could help define the values for a paper mill).

A second difficulty is the translation of values across a large organization. The values held at the corporate level may not make sense for staff located in regional offices or for employees falling outside the core business. I have always been a believer in "group culture," as opposed to "corporate culture." The larger and more diverse the group, the more watered down an organizational culture becomes. Because of this, there are probably only two or three values that could universally apply to all employees in an organization.

Even if the value system is well defined, a practitioner's ability to identify and evaluate fit is limited. Motivation questionnaires can help, but the terminology used in their construction is necessarily broad. For example, a questionnaire may ask how much a candidate values merit-based reward, but the questionnaire does not specifically address whether this reward should be recognized at an individual or group level. A clarifying conversation with the candidate is required, bringing up all the problems addressed in the previous chapter on the quality of interviews for predicting fit (that is, whether someone expresses his or her values truthfully and how these are interpreted by the interviewer).

## Motivated Employees Are Engaged Employees

In the beginning of this chapter, motivation was positioned as a complementary and necessary factor in the relationship between capability and performance. This relationship was stated as a given, but now is an appropriate time to make the connection for how the fulfillment of traits, needs, and values drives behavior. I will argue that this relationship to organizational performance drives most employers' interest in motivation, rather than improving employee well-being.

Despite its logical connection, the relationship between motivation and performance has been difficult to demonstrate experimentally, as it is often unclear whether maximum or typical performance is being measured. Capability is generally thought to be the primary determinant of performance, with motivation differentiating typical and maximum performance (what can be accomplished with a little extra effort). Evidence from real workplaces has found a scattering of support for motivation's effects on absenteeism, commitment, customer service, and organizational citizenship behavior.

More commonly, motivation has been seen as a predictor of satisfaction and engagement (how an employee thinks and feels about the workplace), which affects performance. An indirect relationship has been discovered for a range of performance indicators, from customer service to productivity and accident reduction. For example, Ipsos Mori (2006) and Hay (2001) estimate that engagement accounts for between 20 and 43 percent higher performance. Ipsos Mori also found that the highly engaged are 87 percent less likely to leave voluntarily, whereas Watson Wyatt (2009) report that the engaged miss 43 percent fewer days of work.

To improve performance, organizations have a choice between improving employee ability or their motivation. Ability is the straightforward option, by changing how employees are selected at hiring and the training they receive once on the job. Motivation can also be targeted in recruitment, by identifying the key motivators held by applicants and assessing whether they are likely to be aligned to the workplace. But this is an imperfect science, due to the generic nature of questionnaires and how they are applied to specific jobs, varying competence in how interviewers explore a candidate's motivators, and pressures by employers and candidates to hold back from full disclosure.

As a second option, employers can change the workplace to better motivate employees. Employers seeking change are guided by a rich history of how workplace environments can be fixed to meet the needs of employees. For example, early research involving Scientific Management principles focused on altering the level of pay employees received, while the human relations movement encouraged employees to have a voice in how work was done.

Underlying whether employers think change will be worthwhile is a question of philosophy. Douglas McGregor in 1957 defined two distinct approaches management takes when interacting with employees. Managers who ascribe to Theory X believe that employees are naturally resistant to work and need constant pressure to achieve work objectives. Employee motivation under Theory X involves the avoidance of punishment. In contrast, managers adopting Theory Y believe employees are not lazy, but require direction in how they can be involved in meeting organizational goals. Managers who ascribe to Theory X will likely resist changing the workplace environment when employee motivation wanes, looking to external recruitment as the answer.

Even if a manager believes in Theory Y, his or her ability to change the workplace may be stifled by a lack of organizational support or funding. What is evident from the previous sections is that there is a wide range of needs, traits, and values to address, posing a very practical problem both about what to change and where to begin. From my experience, employers must prioritize the motivators that have the greatest potential to improve the satisfaction and engagement of employees. Addressing hygiene factors, acting ethically, giving employees space to try new things, and defining common organizational values are great places to begin.

What underlies all this is the organization's desire to improve performance, and so motivators are addressed only so far as they drive the organization's objectives. This perspective clashes with the establishment of a solid psychological contract, where both parties' interests are addressed. Psychometrics have the potential to capture enough information to have a balanced conversation, but current practice falls short of addressing motivation purely for the sake of employees. Current practice is to dictate the motivational profile required to perform, rather than looking at the converse—what can change to improve the well-being of employees.

When given a choice between dealing with long-term grievances, such as investing in the workplace, changing how work is assigned, or having difficult conversations with managers who undermine a healthy culture, and changing the profile of who is hired, employers tend to think in the short term. A motivational profile is drawn up and psychometrics are used to identify individuals least likely to be offended by the failing workplace. Although this strategy may suffice when the workplace is dictated by the type of work the organization does (for example, the high pressure environment experienced by ambulance drivers), changing recruitment strategies just postpones the enviable. Either the workplace will hit a new low in reputation or the pipeline of capable staff will dry up, leaving the organization nowhere to go other than to fix the issues that they should have addressed in the first place.

Beyond financial considerations, workplaces that fulfill the motivational needs of employees are simply better environments to be in. The intangible benefit of benevolent employers probably could be linked back to profits and growth, but this would defeat the purpose. The more that I am asked to defend the return on investment of what we do as practitioners, the more I question whether we are missing the point by trying to find a number for everything we do. Workplaces are social environments, with all the benefits and hardships of any other human relationship. I don't think I could or want to attach a monetary value to all my personal relationships. Not only is this unhealthy and likely to lead to some truly strange behavior, but the numbers would be meaningless. Friend X is worth $50,000, as he lives close by, whereas Friend Y is worth $60,000 because she has an extensive collection of my favorite music that I could borrow.

Investment in employees' psychological contract, by understanding and responding to their needs, ensures that both parties work toward mutual ends, even if these ends cannot be clearly defined or articulated. All we need to know is that both parties are going in the same direction, which is a very different perspective on motivation than what is used by most employers today.

## Changes in Motivation with Age and Generations

Although every individual differs in the type of workplace environment that motivates him or her, life span research has identified some commonalities between employees as they age. Employees typically experience a decrease in their ability to perform tasks requiring speed, accuracy, or a high degree of working memory; however, they show growth in their ability to solve problems due to their advanced knowledge and experience. When translating this data to overall job performance, no major relationship has been found between age and performance across the majority of professions.

The effects of aging are more pronounced for employee attitudes. The bulk of the scientific research concludes that overall job satisfaction, job involvement, and organizational commitment increase with age. These trends are driven primarily by how pleased employees are with the work they are conducting, rather than by features of the workplace (for example, satisfaction with their supervisors, workmates, or organizations). The relationship is not linear, with the initial excitement of young employees dropping after a few years and then rebounding to the high level initially experienced.

Driving employee attitudes are generic changes in the motivational profile of employees and how well they are fulfilled. From a *needs* perspective, the change in ability from speed to problem solving results in older employees seeking out work where their knowledge can be used more effectively, at the expense of trying out new experiences. They tend to seek work that is consistent with their self-identity and provides intrinsic gratification. This emphasis on security is not limited to the type of work undertaken, but can also be expressed in the hours worked, the types of employee benefits sought, and support provided by their supervisors or co-workers. Security needs replace younger employees' desires for experience, as characterized by career progression, work variety, self-actualization, and opportunities for socializing.

Although the expression of *traits* are more consistent across an employee's career, extroversion (activity level), neuroticism (anxiety), and openness to experience show some decline with age. This finding is consistent with older workers' desire for security, replacing a need to pursue new experiences.

The expression of *values* on employee behavior shows more variability, especially on what researchers have defined as the "Protestant Work Ethic" (PWE). PWE captures employee beliefs in hard work, rationality, frugality, and individualism. Young workers might adopt PWE as a strategy for achieving greater career progression and professional growth (extrinsic rewards), as well as a means of justifying their investment in education and training. In contrast, older workers may adopt a PWE to drive greater intrinsic satisfaction from their work, irrespective of whether their effort will be rewarded by their employer. In other words, employees at various ages may embrace a strong PWE to rationalize and direct future behaviors, but do so for a variety of reasons.

Equally important for predicting employee motivation are *generational differences*. Before we look at this, what is meant by a "generation" requires definition. Unfortunately, there is little agreement about the demarcation of generational cohorts. For example, in an article by Howe and Strauss (2007), six generations were identified: the GI Generation (born between 1901 and 1924), Silent Generation (born between 1925 and 1942), Baby Boomers (born between 1943 and 1960), Generation X (born between 1961 and 1981), Millennial Generation (born between 1982 and 2005, often called Generation Y), and the Homeland Generation (born between 2006 and 2025). In contrast, Twenge, in her treatise on generational differences, lumps the three youngest generations into a single group, naming her book and the cohort as "Generation Me" (born between 1970 and the present).

Regardless of the title given, a generation shares similar birth years and significant life events, as well as a common geographic location. Howe and Strauss propose that generational profiles are predictable and cycle around four main archetypes. The Baby Boomers represent the "prophet" archetype, which is characterized by value-driven, moralistic, and self-directed behavior. Having experienced life events such as the Vietnam War, the Kennedy Assassination, the Sexual Revolution, and Watergate, the Baby Boomers seek out individual meaning, prestige, and self-sufficiency and, therefore, view retirement as a challenge to their self-identity.

In contrast, Generation X represents the "nomad" archetype, whose members are described as tough, unwanted, adventurous, and cynical of social institutions. Members of this generation are considered effective in pushing efficiency, cutting bureaucracy, and driving innovation. Having experienced rapid change that has resulted in financial, familial, and societal insecurity, Generation X members have adopted an independent approach to the workplace and are willing to switch employers and jobs frequently.

The Millennial Generation represents the "hero" archetype, which is characterized by a return to conventional and institutionally driven behavior, thereby demonstrating a high degree of loyalty and trust. Members of the Millennial Generation are racially and ethnically diverse, technologically savvy, and self-confident. However, this cohort is also characterized by a sheltered upbringing that is likely to result in a high degree of employer dependency.

Not yet seen is the "artist" archetype, which is predicted for the Homeland Generation. This cohort completes the cycle with an emphasis on emotion and compromise that will likely lead to a new cultural awakening of what should be valued in life.

Differences in the social, economic, and political environment are evident in the descriptions of the generations above. These forces have led to characteristics that are held in common by generational members, which include different expectations and attitudes about the workplace. For example, Generation X members are likely to thrive under autonomous working arrangements, determining for themselves the best way for accomplishing a task. In contrast, members of the Millennial Generation are likely to thrive under stronger organizational structures and close supervision. If employers are unable to bridge this transition between autonomous working and high organizational support, the motivation of the Millennial Generation members is likely to be lost.

Although the demographic profile changes in the long term, there are multiple generations working at any given point in time, with different needs, traits, and values that can be in conflict with each other. At present, there are three generations employed in the workplace (Baby Boomer, Generation X, and Millennial), each expecting employers to react to their generational preferences.

From a *needs* perspective, Baby Boomers seek out positions that convey high social status, whereas Generation X members prefer to work in roles with loose structures and where individual discretion is allowed for how work is accomplished. The Millennials are motivated by roles that offer quick job progression, immediate gratification, self-expression, and variety. However, this generation is also characterized by needs for a high degree of organizational support, recognition, and feedback.

Regarding *traits*, Baby Boomers demonstrate tendencies for introspection and self-absorption, whereas Generation X members prefer pragmatism and flexibility. Traits discovered for the Millennials include a high degree of self-confidence, optimism, trust, and risk aversion. These traits are complementary to the generational needs already discussed and together drive Baby Boomers to seek out meaning in their work, Generation X members to strive for autonomy, and Millennials to pursue work environments that they believe will bring them the greatest fulfillment.

*Values* are also influenced by generational cohort. Baby Boomers have been found to value material success, self-sufficiency, and tradition, while Generation X members emphasize decisions made by sound logic, meritocracy, and the distribution of power. The Millennials demonstrate both pro-social and selfish tendencies. This generational cohort values ethnic, gender, and experiential diversity in the workplace and seeks to gain from the variety it brings. However, Millennials are ultimately driven by a feeling of entitlement for emotional and physical gratification that can sometimes interfere with the promotion of a positive workplace environment.

A summary of generational and aging trends on motivation is displayed in Figure 4.5. For those of you familiar with the American version of the television show *The Office,* the trends can be represented by some of the main characters. Phyllis represents the Baby Boomer, who attempts to maintain her status in the office and values tradition, especially when it comes to office party planning. Jim represents Generation X, taking huge discretion in how he goes about his work, taking liberty in harassing Dwight on occasion. The Millennial of the pack is Ryan, who believes he is ready for an executive-level position, following a very successful internship.

In sum, motivation is in constant flux. At the individual level, the mix and importance of specific needs, traits, and values changes as an individual ages. At a broad social level, the way employees

| | | Needs | Traits | Values |
|---|---|---|---|---|
| **Age** | **Early Career** | • Career Progression<br>• Work Variety<br>• Socializing | • Extroverted<br>• Focused on Self<br>• Open to Experience | • Instrumentality of Work |
| | **Late Career** | • Physical Security<br>• Predictability<br>• Managerial Support | • Introverted<br>• Socially Oriented<br>• Prefer Routine | • High Work Ethic<br>• Pride in Craft<br>• Intrinsic Value of Work |
| **Generation** | **Millennial** | • Progression<br>• Self-Expression<br>• Variety<br>• Managerial Support | • Confident<br>• Optimistic<br>• Trusting<br>• Risk Adverse | • Diversity<br>• Personal Gratification |
| | **Generation X** | • Loose Structure<br>• Discretion in Work | • Pragmatic<br>• Flexible | • Logic<br>• Meritocracy<br>• Distribution of Power |
| | **Baby Boomer** | • Status<br>• Prestige | • Introspected<br>• Self-Absorbed | • Material Success<br>• Self-Sufficiency<br>• Tradition |

FIGURE 4.5 Summary of Age and Generation Trends for Motivation

engage with their workplace is shaped by significant, shared life events. Practitioners are challenged to find strategies that balance the individual and group in fulfilling needs, allowing for the expression of traits, and altering organizational values. At stake is a company's ability to attract, recruit, and engage employees with the right skills and experience. The sharpest tools in a practitioner's toolbox are the psychometrics that provide a glimpse into employee desires. The trick is to persuade organizations to appreciate the power of psychometrics and to ensure that they are consistently and appropriately used.

## Restoring the Balance with Person–Environment Fit

Over the past decade, practitioners have begun to take notice of the concept of *person-environment fit* as a fuller way to express how well motivators are fulfilled by employers. Although this interest may have waned slightly after the economic downturn (as has interest in employee engagement in general), fit provides a mechanism to summarize the relationship between an employee and their workplace. Fit is defined as occurring whenever at least one entity (person or organization) provides what the other requires or when the employee and organization share certain fundamental characteristics in common.

Unlike traditional measures of motivation, like the psychometrics discussed earlier, fit measures capture both what the individual desires and what is offered within the organization. Fit can be assessed across five different levels, specifically the job, group, supervisor, organization, and vocation levels. The term *person-environment fit* represents the aggregate alignment between the employee and his or her workplace across levels, but often the amount of fit can vary significantly between them. For example, an employee could enjoy both her job and vocation, but experience a misfit with her supervisor, workgroup, and organization, leading to an overall poor person-environment fit.

The dimensions of fit across levels are diverse and include beliefs, attitudes, values, personality, and demographics. To help make sense of this range of dimensions, a distinction is made between two types of fit: *supplementary* and *complementary*. Supplementary fit is described as a relationship that embellishes shared goals, values, norms, personality, or attitudes between an individual and his or her co-workers. In contrast, complementary fit occurs when the relationship is made whole when the needs of either the employee or organization are fulfilled by the other party. For the employee, the organization can provide rewards, learning, or other motivators (termed *needs-supplies*), whereas the employee can provide the organization with knowledge or skills (termed *demands-abilities*). The distinction between the two is important for predicting the outcomes of alignment between employees and their workplace, as demands-abilities fit is related to performance, while needs-supplies fit influences satisfaction and organizational citizenship behavior.

During recruitment, applicants actively seek out information about their potential workplace and evaluate fit based on the credibility of the source. For example, an applicant is likely to view a recommendation by a recruitment agency more skeptically than a recommendation from a close friend. In terms of the content used to evaluate fit, applicants generally focus on the organization's culture and role requirements when evaluating a job offer.

Organizations, too, evaluate fit, especially when selecting from a pool of qualified candidates. Organizations tend to seek out valid and objective data on the values, skills, abilities, and personality characteristics of candidates as a means of evaluating fit. Interviews are crucial to this process, allowing for open questions, feedback when assumptions are wrong, and probing by both candidates and the recruiter to come to a hiring decision. Across interview stages, emphasis shifts from person-job fit (Can the individual fulfill job requirements?) to person-organization fit (Will the individual fit in here?) before a final decision is made.

Once an applicant accepts a job offer and becomes an employee, a process of mutual adjustment begins, with perceptions of fit leading to increased alignment through socialization. Schneider's Attraction-Selection-Attrition (ASA) model suggests that initial perceptions of fit are strengthened in a self-fulfilling way, whereby complementary goals are actively sought out and misfits weeded out through rejection by other organizational members. For employees who demonstrate a high degree of fit, the personal and organizational benefits of employee satisfaction, commitment, organizational citizenship behavior, and retention are expected.

No consistent method of measuring person-environment fit is adopted universally. Rather, three main types of criteria are used, specifically *subjective*, *perceived*, and *objective* fit. Subjective fit is found by asking employees directly whether they fulfill job requirements or share group and organizational values in common. Perceived fit is determined by asking employees about the skills they bring to the organization, as well as their individual desires. This information is then compared to what the employee perceives the organization as providing. Objective fit is considered the strongest measure of person-environment fit, wherein self-described skills and needs are compared to independent information about what is provided for in the workplace.

The use of questionnaires to measure person-environment fit is a less common approach than the use of interviews that qualitatively explore the employment relationship. Whether questionnaires or interviews are used, practitioners must decide how to summarize the degree of person-environment fit for a given employee. Single-score measures are commonly used, due to their simplicity, but they are thought to discard information, conceal sources of fit, and restrict prediction of outcomes. Alternatively, the dimensions of person-environment fit can be kept separate, allowing for the identification of individuals sharing common needs and predictions about the motivators that have the greatest potential to increase engagement and satisfaction.

On the whole, person-environment fit tools have the potential to effectively unearth the drivers of candidates, such that better decisions can be made by both the employee and the company about whether the relationship is on solid ground. Information is captured about what the employee desires, as well as what the company provides, using a common vocabulary to summarize the quality of the relationship. This is an improvement on what current psychometrics accomplish, which consider the employee in isolation from the workplace. And they are definitely a better alternative to the various personality instruments circulating around the Internet with no scientific backing whatsoever.

The real question is whether the improved information captured by person-environment fit (Figure 4.6) measures will lead to better organizational practices. This is where I am far less optimistic. New tools, no matter how strong, do not fundamentally change the power difference between employers and their staff. Organizations tend to take a short-term strategy of focusing on motivators that have a direct link to performance, selecting candidates with an agreed-on profile in mind (holding true to the company mantra, while not being offended by any cultural quirks). The individual needs of the employee, which fall outside of the company-sponsored profile, are discussed halfheartedly or not all at by employers, who might follow targeted scripts in interviews, promotion discussions, and appraisals. However, these forgotten motivators may be driving an individual's behavior in the workplace and, without them being attended to, the links in the psychological contract can break down.

Worse still, I have come into contact with a number of organizations that use motivation as a means of screening candidates for hiring or promotion, with little or no validation with the candidate. Assumptions are made that if an individual is not motivated by a particular feature of the workplace, he or she is likely to act in a way that is contrary to the workplace culture, with knock-on effects on performance. But this argument is tenuous, as we all do things that sit outside of our preferences.

For example, I do not particularly enjoy waking up early in the morning for a business meeting, but if the meeting is of crucial

| | |
|---|---|
| **Level** | • Vocation |
| | • Organization |
| | • Group |
| | • Supervisor |
| | • Job |
| **Type** | • Supplementary |
| | • Complementary (Demands-Abilities or Needs-Supplies |
| **Measurement** | • Subjective |
| | • Perceived |
| | • Objective |

FIGURE 4.6　Key Characteristics of Person–Environment Fit

importance, of course I'll be there. Relying on questionnaire results to screen candidates does not allow for such inconsistencies (the motivators of sleeping in and impressing my boss are in conflict). If you had no clue about my motivation to impress my boss, you would have predicted that I would either sleep in, turn up late, or act grumpy for the duration of the meeting. The equation *Performance = Capability x Motivation* is not in question here, but rather which motivators will win out in driving performance.

In sum, the measurement of motivation provides a complementary perspective to tests of ability, capturing separately what an individual *can* and *will* achieve. Yet the relationship is not always straightforward and can lead to a variety of workplace behaviors. Organizations often take a linear approach, targeting specific motivational profiles that they believe are linked to performance. Without validating the results of the tools, questioning how they might play out in the real workplace environment, and exploring whether other motivators will override the relationship, the organization will not benefit from the insight these tools provide about an employee's fit to the workplace. As practitioners, we can push harder to ensure that employee motivators are heard, understood, and acted upon, for the benefit of the organization and employee alike.

# Chapter 5

# Employee Development

A lot goes into a healthy employment relationship. Both the employee and the employer have responsibility to fulfill the other's needs in a reciprocal arrangement. Employees perform for the employer by using skills and knowledge that they have gained both on the job and prior to employment. In turn, the employer fulfills the motivational needs of employees and allows them a degree of self-determination in how they go about their jobs.

In the last chapter, I briefly touched on a third component of person-environment fit, specifically, the elements of the employment relationship that are not reciprocal, but held in common. *Supplementary fit* occurs when an employment relationship embellishes the shared goals, values, norms, personality, or attitudes between an individual and his or her workmates. It literally is the oil that greases the wheel of what would otherwise be a transactional relationship between a worker and his or her employer.

When employees identify strongly with their employer, take pride in their work, and feel that they are moving in the same direction, good things happen. Employees stick around longer, invest more heavily in their jobs, and are willing to weather a personal setback. The self-interest inherent to *complementary fit,* where one party expects the other to fulfill his or her needs, does not go nearly far enough to ensure a long-term and sustainable employment relationship.

One way to ensure that employees feel valued and connected to each other is to offer targeted personal development. When employers reset what is valued in the organization, help employees fit in, and provide tools that will enable them to work more effectively with their peers, employees recognize that their organization is dedicated to a long-term relationship.

In this chapter, I will use the model of the psychological contract to frame how development can transform the employment relationship. This will be especially useful for the discussion in the next chapter, when we look at how change without sufficient development can go awry and fundamentally break employees' connection with their workplace.

We will look at three components of a typical development program. The first involves building *self-awareness* of developmental needs, accomplished through some form of assessment, from performance feedback to workplace simulations and psychometrics. By gaining insight into how their capabilities and competencies compare to those of their peers, employees can focus their learning on activities that have the greatest benefit. A 2011 survey of HR practitioners representing 463 global organizations discovered that assessments were used in 64 percent of career development programs and 49 percent of skills audits. A follow-up study found a similar result, with 62 percent of companies conducting formal assessments and 54 percent using self-identification of development needs.

After their awareness has been raised, employees undergo some form of developmental challenge. This could be focused on raising technical skills (such as degree or certification programs, formalized in-company training, and self-directed development through reading books or engaging with professional organizations), gaining new experience (through job rotations and stints in different parts of the business), or establishing new behavioral habits (through action learning, stretch assignments, and role modeling).

Companies don't treat these types of development challenges equally, relying instead on traditional classroom training. In 2000, for example, the American Society for Training and Development found that close to 80 percent of development relied on classroom training as the primary delivery channel. The tide has changed since then (the same survey in 2013 found that level dropping to 54 percent). However, the profession has a long way to go to reach the Center for Creative Leadership's suggestion that 70 percent of development should be experiential, 20 percent based on feedback and observation, and only 10 percent coming from formalized training.

The final component occurs alongside the development challenge. *Organizational support* in the form of *mentoring* (to solidify gains in skills or knowledge) and *coaching* (to embed behavioral change) is essential for ensuring a safe psychological environment for growth. A huge amount of interest in business coaching has occurred this past decade. A report by CEB in 2004 found that approximately 50 percent of organizations surveyed had utilized executive coaching in the past eighteen months, with 70 percent of those organizations believing that it was more effective than training for increasing performance.

These three components, self-awareness, development challenge, and organizational support, can effectively realign an employee with the workplace and renew the psychological contract. Too often the results fall short of this outcome and may actually do harm to the employment relationship. Data intended to increase self-awareness is sometimes repurposed to make decisions about promotions and work assignments. Development challenges are often limited to a few options that are most aligned to organizational needs, rather than recognizing the personal desires of employees. Also, employees may not be given the opportunity to fail, contrary to the goals of providing a safe and supportive learning environment. Practitioners have the ability to change all of this, providing yet another battleground for improving how talent is managed.

## Psychological Contract

The psychological contract is an incredibly powerful model for describing the glue that binds employees to their workplace. An understanding of the content behind the relationship and how deep the connections go can help to predict whether employees will contribute above and beyond expectations, share innovative ideas, and accept change when it comes their way. If the glue is not strong enough, employees can withdraw from those around them, or worse, work to sabotage the company's performance.

When the term *psychological contract* was first coined in the early 1960s, it was broadly defined as a set of mutual expectations held by the employee and his or her employer that are played out in day-to-day interactions. The expectations making up the psychological contract can be explicit (such as those written in an offer of employment), implied (for example, adhering to professional work standards), or even unrecognized by both parties (for example, similar preferences about socializing or the appropriateness of humor).

Over time, practitioners refined their definitions, noting that psychological contracts are in constant flux and change in response to the expectations held by either the employee or the employer. A popular definition was provided by Rousseau in 2004, who said that psychological contracts are "beliefs, based upon promises expressed or implied, regarding an exchange agreement between an individual and, in organizations, the employing firm and its agents." This employee-centric viewpoint has been criticized for discounting the employer's perspective, which I agree is a problem. Contracts imply mutually to both parties and, because of this, the perspectives of both the employee and his or her employer are valid for understanding the quality of the relationship.

But the question is: Who represents the organization in the employment relationship? Conceivably, it could be an organizational founder, hiring manager, recruiter, or any other company representative that the employee has had meaningful conversations with. It is easy to assume that the line manager holds the psychological contract, but if this person is distant, involved late in the hiring process, or hard to connect with, the employee may see someone else as his or her contractual counterpart. If the core contract holder is not recognized, the engagement of staff can be lost in an instant when expectations are not fulfilled.

Psychological contracts are broadly accepted to differ from traditional employee contracts in that they are unwritten, contain both implicit and explicit features, have no legal bearing, and can extend beyond the immediate job.

The formation of psychological contracts can be particularly challenging for an organization to control, in comparison with typical employment contracts. From the moment that an applicant comes into contact with a prospective employer, the psychological contract starts to take form. Initially, applicants seek information about what they can expect from their potential employer, soak in information from career portals, advice from job incumbents, their own experience as customers, overt promises made by advertisements or recruiters, and, increasingly, anonymous reviews about the quality of the workplace (glassdoor.com).

When someone is hired, this process intensifies, as the employee begins to integrate his or her direct experiences into the psychological contract, which can include the treatment received from a manager and co-workers, how much support is available when learning the job, and whether promises made during recruitment are kept.

Quality interactions that explicitly address the obligations held by both parties lessen the chance of misunderstanding and a premature ending of the employment relationship. More experienced employees tend to be better at identifying and managing any disconnects in the psychological contract, before they spin out of control.

Once established, employees begin to monitor the psychological contract to see whether obligations are being fulfilled. As the employee becomes more comfortable with his or her role and the organization, monitoring diminishes unless a contract breach is experienced. As will be addressed in the next chapter, psychological contracts end when the needs of either party change fundamentally from what has been established, which can result in either a renegotiation of the contract or a separation of employment.

So far, I've discussed how a psychological contract forms, but not the content that underlies it. In general, employees expect companies to provide training, work-life balance, consultation in times of change, discretion about how work is performed, recognition and pay for performance, a safe and congenial environment, fairness and respect, employee benefits, and job security. In exchange, employees are held responsible for working their contracted hours, good quality workmanship, honesty in internal and external interactions, loyalty, respect in the treatment of property, professionalism, and flexibility in work assignments.

Two fundamental types of obligations can be distinguished within the above mix. *Transactional obligations*, such as pay or working contracted hours, are economic in nature, have formal terms, focus on the short term, and are made explicit. In contrast, *relational obligations*, such as fairness and loyalty, are based on trust, leave room for flexibility, focus on the long term, and are often implicit (not discussed openly). Interestingly, employees tend to focus on transactional obligations, whereas organizations stress the relational.

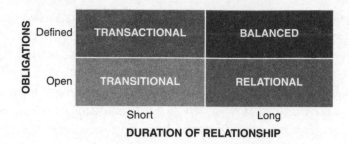

FIGURE **5.1** Four Different Types of Psychological Contracts

The unique combination of obligations held in an employment relationship will flavor the overall psychological contract, splitting it into four basic categories (Figure 5.1):

◆ *Transactional:* A tit-for-tat relationship, good as long as both parties hold up their sides of the bargain.
◆ *Relational:* A pleasant place to work; however, it may be unclear exactly what the employee is there to do.
◆ *Balanced:* A mixture of transactional and relational, where both parties feel committed to each other and hold the other accountable.
◆ *Transitional:* A temporary relationship with a very limited scope, for example, a contractor providing maternity leave coverage.

The two forms of *complementary fit* discussed in the last chapter, where organizations provide rewards and other motivators in exchange for knowledge and skills, fall more closely into the transactional obligations of the psychological contract. They are explicit, traded independently, firmly established at the time of hiring, and often can be monitored for fulfillment. Moreover, the exchange of performance for reward can occur over a relatively short period of time with no assumption about a long-term investment in the employment relationship.

*Supplemental fit* is different, capturing features like goals, values, attitudes, and behavioral norms that are harder to pin down and monitor. Falling into the relational obligations of the psychological contract, they represent the overall quality of the employment relationship and how likely it is to survive conflict. It is not so much about trading for self-interest, as about fulfilling priorities held in common and a belief that both parties are working toward a common future.

In its purest form, employee development is an investment in the psychological contract by heightening supplementary fit. This is not to say that development cannot be dragged into a transactional exchange, for example, when an employee threatens to leave the company unless he is enrolled in an executive MBA program. Rather, the act of investing in employees connotes that they are valued and trusted, with the relationship expected to endure for the long term.

Occasional realignment through development reaffirms the shared purpose of the organization and reminds employees about what they are tasked to do. This is especially true when there is a high degree of employee consultation in developing learning content, such as in training best practices or sharing case studies. By beginning with some form of assessment, employees can gage how far away they are from the organizational norm and thereby determine how much development is appropriate. Through support structures and a psychologically safe environment, employees can realign to a new way of working that is held in common with their peers.

Effective development programs renew the psychological contract by reinforcing shared company values, establishing where the employee fits in, and providing the tools necessary to deliver. How well typical development programs perform against this standard will form much of the commentary over the following three sections. I will argue that development programs often are subverted away from their intended purpose and. therefore, have minimal impact on supplemental fit.

## Assessment for Development

Gaining insight into what one does well and not so well forms the basis from which any personal development plan is built. Feedback can take a variety of shapes, from formalized assessments (such as 360-degree feedback) to comments made during day-to-day interactions with co-workers. Feedback can come from managers, peers, direct reports, customers, professional coaches, or even an automated assessment system.

Regardless of the source, feedback directs employees to seek out new skills and experiences or to change their workplace behavior (aka competencies). Yet, the link between self-awareness and improvement can be lost depending on whether employees feel in control, understand the importance of change, and maintain their self-confidence.

Not all employees are equal in how they seek feedback, with individuals taking either an active or a passive role in their development. Active feedback seekers elicit opinions from their co-workers and thus control the timing of when insight is gained. Alternatively, passive feedback seekers monitor the workplace environment for indications about their performance (that is, take part in business reviews or appraisals), but do not actively ask others for their opinions.

Although the information gained by active feedback seekers is known to surpass that gained by their passive peers, it is understandable why some individuals avoid seeking feedback completely. Active feedback seeking can be viewed as a sign of weakness, insecurity, and incompetence. It is particularly shunned by employees who have high levels of self-esteem, a strong tolerance for ambiguity, and frequent social encounters in the workplace.

Beyond the insight gained by feedback they receive, active feedback seekers benefit from a stronger personal brand, but only if they seek critical feedback (not just the kudos that stroke the ego). Critical feedback seekers have been shown to be more highly regarded than their passive peers and seen as genuinely motivated to drive personal and organizational performance.

Due to the importance of self-awareness for personal development, it is no wonder that practitioners attempt to force the issue for those who do not actively seek feedback. Practitioners may attempt to change the work culture by increasing a manager's tolerance of mistakes, encouraging cautious risk taking, and providing support when things go wrong. More heavy-handed approaches focus on implementing a formalized process for gaining objective, constructive feedback about employees.

Such a program is not the same as actively seeking feedback, because employees have lost the control and timing of the feedback. Before commenting on the effectiveness of self-awareness programs, I want to spend a few minutes addressing the common methodologies and tools used by practitioners for raising self-awareness across large groups of employees.

Any of the tools discussed in the previous chapters could theoretically be included in a self-awareness program, providing varying degrees of useful information on an individual's strengths and development needs. Audits of skills or experience provide very tangible recommendations about the gaps that need to be filled in order to perform a job effectively. Although captured at the time of hiring through structured application forms or entered into an applicant tracking system, the quality of information about employees degrades rapidly as they move from position to position within a company. Probably, the most to up-to-date records will be formalized company training records, especially when ongoing certification or registration is required. With a significant change in strategy or implementation of a new capability framework, a skills needs analysis is sometimes performed. Although effective at cleaning up employee records, these can be a significant time sink for the organization.

Performance ratings provide another perspective, hitting home the importance of development for career advancement and reward, as well as for identifying the relative priority of different development interventions for their impact on key activities. As will be discussed in the next chapter, the quality of performance appraisals varies significantly, depending on both the measurability of job outcomes (whether they can be objectively observed over regular time intervals) and the proficiency of managers to accurately appraise employees.

Measures of motivation, with psychometrics aimed at employee needs, traits, or values, provide insight into an individual's eagerness to develop. Often referred to as measures of *potential*, psychometrics can help predict whether a development program will be good for employees (are they being asked to do something they enjoy doing), as well as their potential speed in learning the new material. Of course, we all willingly go through development that we find boring (personally, I wish I had back the three hours I invested this year in training for a new time and expense system), but any sustained change requires motivation to implement.

The last of our five key ingredients, *behavioral competencies*, requires special attention in this discussion on self-awareness. Many practitioners in my field argue that behaviors are the lynchpin for determining the success of any development intervention. Capabilities (skills and experience) and motivation come together through the behavior that an employee exhibits on the job, which, with a favorable environment, leads to the attainment of key activities. It is only when an employee puts training into practice that the payoffs of development programs are felt.

With such a pivotal role ascribed to behavior, it is no wonder so much is invested on creating tools to heighten an employee's self-awareness. As mentioned earlier, workplace simulations can provide insight on behaviors, and there is no shortage of companies assembling exercises (role plays, presentations, in-trays, group exercises, written exercises) into *development centers*. This title is a misnomer, as very little development occurs at the actual center. Assessment is conducted, personalized reports are drafted, and feedback sessions are given, all aimed at increasing self-awareness.

More prevalent for increasing self-awareness of behavioral competencies, 360-degree feedback surveys gather and deliver feedback from multiple individuals across a range of relationships (such as line managers, peers, direct reports, and outside parties). It is estimated that, since 1992, $152 million has been spent annually on 360-degree feedback programs, with nearly universal support for the technique in Fortune 500 companies. In practice, 360-degree feedback tools are not used in isolation, in conjunction with psychometrics or development centers.

360-degree feedback tools can send a clear message to employees about what behaviors are valued in the culture. It is no surprise that 70 percent of companies that have adopted 360-degree feedback are using the tool as a vehicle for embedding a specific corporate culture. When performed across multiple years, alignment can be tracked and further development interventions planned. Increasingly, organizations are including results in the formalized appraisal process or using them as a means of tracking the attainment of objectives set by line managers.

Although 360-degree feedback is said to increase on-the-job performance, decrease development needs, and improve customer service, these outcomes are not guaranteed. At times, 360-degree feedback has hindered organizations. A key factor is whether employees perceived

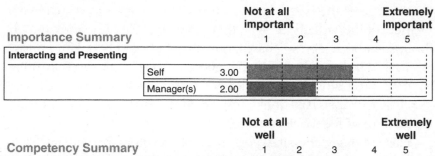

| Importance Summary | | | Not at all important | | | | Extremely important |
|---|---|---|---|---|---|---|---|
| | | | 1 | 2 | 3 | 4 | 5 |
| Interacting and Presenting | | | | | | | |
| | Self | 3.00 | | | | | |
| | Manager(s) | 2.00 | | | | | |

| Competency Summary | | | Not at all well | | | | Extremely well |
|---|---|---|---|---|---|---|---|
| | | | 1 | 2 | 3 | 4 | 5 |
| Interacting and Presenting | | | | | | | |
| Communicating with, persuading and influencing others. | Self | 3.55 | | | | | |
| | Manager(s) | 2.00 | | | | | |
| | Colleagues | 3.41 | | | | | |
| | Direct reports | 3.45 | | | | | |
| | Others | 3.59 | | | | | |

Figure 5.2 Sample Output from a 360-Degree Feedback Report

*Source:* SHL, 360-Degree Feedback Report, courtesy of CEB. © 2014 SHL, a part of CEB. All rights reserved. Used with permission.

the feedback (Figure 5.2) as task-based or as a personal attack. If the feedback threatens employees' self-esteem or is outside their personal control, performance will drop.

Only if employees strongly identify with the organization, share in its values, and believe that they have the ability to affect work outcomes will the self-awareness gained by receiving the feedback translate into performance improvements. Goals play an intermediary role, whereby an appropriate standard of behavior is identified from the feedback and formalized into a personal development plan.

Beyond issues of control, views about the importance or necessity of behavioral change can affect the effort individuals exert following their feedback. When behavioral change is deemed necessary, recipients tend to view the feedback positively, listen attentively to its messages, view change as feasible, and set tangible goals. How favorable or unfavorable the feedback is can also affect subsequent performance improvement. The greatest amount of change occurs with those employees rated as poor to moderate performers or, in other words, those with the greatest amount of work to accomplish to close their gaps in performance.

Because of the hard-hitting nature of 360-degree feedback, when a variety of individuals (all with their own agendas) provide opinions about somebody else's behavior, great care should be taken in using this tool. Whenever I engage in a 360 project, I think carefully about how the program is communicated, its timing in the business (not too close to appraisals), the access given to results, and the appropriate training of feedback providers.

I also strongly encourage organizations to allow participants some flexibility in who they nominate and to provide an opt out if the employee feels uncomfortable taking part. 360-degree feedback is probably the most valuable tool for gaining self-awareness, but only if the conditions are right for the message to be heard and accepted.

In general, the right mix of tools can be highly effective at raising self-awareness. We can obtain a view of an employee's preferences, skill gaps, and typical ways of working, all of which can be pulled together into a highly effective and personalized development plan. Where the practice falls short is in how these tools are applied in a typical development program.

First, there are issues around confidentiality and data use. After gaining all this incredible insight into the flaws of your co-workers, it is hard not to think of this information when important people decisions are made. Often out of context and not related to the original scope of the development program, uncovered weaknesses can be used against employees when considering promotions, divvying up salary increases, or assigning new work responsibilities. Worse still, I have witnessed organizations granting access to assessment results to managers not on the list originally communicated to participants.

I have also seen companies conduct development centers prior to major changes in the business, withholding the true intentions of the program from participants. Far from personal development, the assessments were used to weed out those who would no longer fit the new business model. For sure, assessments can be used during restructuring, but they should be implemented in a way consistent with best practice in selection and with full disclosure to participants about the reasons for their use.

Second, self-awareness programs are often a sheep dip. Whether or not employees want to participate, they are either directly forced to undergo assessment or indirectly encouraged through peer pressure. From the discussion above, it is clear that such actions can cause a great deal of harm to employees, especially when there is a hostile work environment, lack of personal control, or the participant suffers from low self-confidence.

Early in my career, I was forced into completing a self-awareness program, which was an annual event in my division. The problem was that I had only worked in the company for three months. The quality of the feedback was marginal, as most of my co-workers did not know me well enough to spot a pattern in behavior. Moreover, I was not in a good psychological state to receive the feedback. I had not reached full competence in my job and was still proving myself. The end result was that I focused overly on the areas for improvement, failing to see any of the positives. My confidence took a major hit. In retrospect, I learned a great deal from this experience, realizing that the timing was incredibly poor and that others should not be subjected to the same practice.

Third, the power relationship is heavily slanted to the organization with self-awareness programs. The criteria used to measure a participant against is based on the competencies and capabilities deemed important by the organization for performance. A tertiary amount of time may be spent on motivation, but only to understand what is standing in the way of improved performance. In some ways this is understandable, as the employer foots the bill for development programs. Yet, the psychological contract would suggest mutual interest in the other party. Investment in the other party is sometimes purely to strengthen the bonds of the relationship, rather than for short-term outcomes that benefit only one side.

If the self-awareness program is allowed to wander, the participants may discover opportunities within their organization that they were not aware of or felt were outside their grasp. I think it is often better to encourage a broader career conversation than to limit the scope to an employee's immediate role and level. Through encouragement, an employer invests in the relational side of the psychological contract, driving an employee's interest and engagement in the workplace.

We'll return to these concerns later in this chapter, after looking at the development opportunities and support structures organizations offer to their workers. It will become evident that employee development has great potential to ensure a strong psychological contract, if practitioners are able to put the right programs in place.

## Developmental Challenges

As mentioned in this chapter's introduction, there is no shortage of employee development options. Instead of rattling off a laundry list of the different types of programs and interventions, I find it easier to focus on what the development is trying to accomplish, falling back on what I consider the five ingredients of any job. I believe that development primarily focuses on improving technical skill, gaining new experience, or establishing new behavioral habits.

To increase their skills, employees enroll in a formalized training program in a given skill area. They may take classes at a local university or through correspondence, leading to a degree, diploma, or certificate. For those of us who are accredited by a professional body, continuous professional development standards are mandated on an annual cycle, which are fulfilled by attending conferences, undergoing peer reviews, taking on self-study, or completing recertification training.

More typically, employees are required to attend company-organized training that aligns to core business processes. On one end of the spectrum, information about new products, policies, or workflows is rolled into an online module that can be viewed at an employee's discretion. This type of training tends to be unoriginal and dry, concerned more about communicating key information, rather than audience engagement.

For example, when the Financial Services Authority came into existence in the UK, I had to undergo a series of e-learning modules on the different regulations, as I was working for a major insurance broker. Each module lasted between thirty and sixty minutes, was text-heavy with virtually no use of multi-media, and tested my knowledge regularly to prove that I was competent on the material. Failure to pass the quiz resulted in a complete restart on the material, which was a great incentive to drink copious amounts of coffee to keep my attention high.

On the other side of the internal training spectrum, blended learning programs combine online material with face-to-face instruction.

One of my favorite consultancy engagements involved the design and delivery of a negotiation training program for commercial buyers, where we used the combination of pre-course work, slide presentations, case studies, and role plays to drive home the course content.

Nowadays, webinars have replaced presentations, while serious games have gained momentum against low-tech training exercises. These replacements offer scale and efficiency, but I am unconvinced that they are as effective as face-to-face training. Skilled trainers can react to the audience, amending the content as they go to captivate and engage, which cannot be replicated by high-tech alternatives.

In the context of a training course, a case study or role play provides a bite-sized experience for employees to try out the content they have just learned. This is not the same as the second type of development challenge, which is geared at providing novel experiences that are long in duration and rich in content. Through job rotations or organized stints in different parts of the business, employees gain an immersive experience that heightens knowledge across a broad range of topics and encourages an understanding of others' roles and frustrations.

Across my career, I have encountered organizations that sponsor customer awareness days, where head office staff are required to work on the front line, to see for themselves what customers think about the company's service. I have also been involved in organizing graduate programs where staff experience a three- to six-month sample of a variety of business areas, before choosing a permanent placement. At the professional level, I have coordinated managerial rotations between business units that are not working effectively together, and even placements into client organizations, for staff to see for themselves what the buyer requires. As you can see, these programs are wide-ranging and can address multiple development needs.

The investment in a well-executed job rotation, where a participant is immersed in a novel and rich work experience, is considered worth the effort. When asked about the effectiveness of different types of development interventions, 76 percent of HR practitioners rated them as most effective, beating out both coaching programs (at 70 percent) and blended learning (at 54 percent).

CEB agrees. In research directly pitting job assignments against formalized training, on-the-job learning was found to be three times more effective for raising performance and improving employees' attitudes toward work. The net benefits equated to a 30 percent increase in performance and 2.6 times greater worker engagement for organizations with on-the-job learning offerings. Shockingly, these results were discovered despite the fact that formalized training is four times more expensive to conduct than on-the-job learning, when factors such as travel, course design, and instructor time are accounted for.

As mentioned, job rotations and assignments can take a variety of shapes, from broadening an employee's perspective of customer and colleague needs, to harmonizing a common way of working across a large organization. Yet, some experiences have been found to uniformly benefit employees aspiring to take on leadership positions. In 2002, McCall and Hollenback suggested that leaders require experience to learn how to effectively respond to cultural differences, run a business, manage others, and handle problematic relationships, as well as gaining an appreciation of leadership qualities and insight on their own styles. Building upon this work and others, CEB suggested in 2006 that well-rounded leaders should experience:

- ◆ *Job transitions* with unfamiliar responsibilities in a new function or geography, where the employee must re-establish his or her reputation
- ◆ *Important tasks* such as creating organizational change by setting direction and fixing inherited problems, taking on greater responsibility when the stakes are high and there is a risk of failure, or managing non-authority relationships
- ◆ *Overcoming obstacles* that have the potential to cause long-term damage to the leader and the business
- ◆ *Support and reflection* on past achievements and failures through personalized feedback and the opportunity to learn from a manager, coach, or mentor

The quality of the experience matters a great deal. A job rotation will only be meaningful if the participant is exposed to novel problems, different customers, or new ways of working. To ensure that the investment in experience is not wasted, many of my clients employ staff to provide oversight in selecting learning opportunities, as well as to manage the end-to-end engagement. Regular check-ins are made with the employee to ensure that the learning is going according to plan. As you can imagine, such oversight is usually reserved for employees in a high potential or leadership program, which limits how far development through new experience can realistically extend.

It is no surprise that many organizations have focused on what can be done within an individual's current role. Employees can be challenged to try new ways of tackling their existing job responsibilities and, by doing so, undergo *behavioral change,* the third type of development. By instilling new habits, individuals can increase their job proficiency, make fewer errors, and align more strongly with the organizational culture. The company's competency framework can be used as a guide and, when it accurately expresses the cultural glue, this structure can point employees in the right direction about where they should invest their energies. Also, everyone has an esoteric bad habit or two that, if identified and worked on, could improve how they interact with their co-workers.

Establishing a new habit requires a fair bit of effort and tends to follow a predictable path. Early on, an employee may be unaware of what "good" looks like for a given competency, which is referred to by Gordon Training International (2014) as *unconscious incompetence.* Once they are aware of their shortcomings and begin thinking through what they could be doing differently, employees reach the stage of *conscious incompetence.* Over time, they gain confidence and skill at exhibiting the target behavior, attaining *conscious competence.* The final stage in the process is when the new behavior becomes a habit, termed *unconscious competence.*

If no more is required from the employee, his or her behavior is likely to hit a plateau of performance. For example, a person working on presenting to large groups may develop to the point of effectively giving a talk driven by PowerPoint about a subject he or she is familiar with. Whether the person will continue in his or her development to become a master orator, like Tony Blair or Bill Clinton, depends in part on personal motivation and what is required in the role. This trend, originally brought up by Fitts and Posner, is popularly referred to as the "OK plateau of acceptable performance." The employee's behavior is good enough to meet immediate needs, but not strong enough to set him or her apart as an expert.

To go beyond the OK plateau requires the learning cycle to begin afresh, by bringing aspects of behavior that are in unconscious incompetence into awareness. Such continuous learning is an effortful process, requiring a constant refinement of behavior with only incremental improvement. Ericsson stresses that practice needs to be deliberate, by focusing on technique, staying goal oriented, and using constant, immediate feedback to push performance further.

In a similar vein, Csikszentmihlyi describes the feeling when the challenge of practice is in optimal balance with the individual's level of skill, terming this the "psychological state of flow." The activity is hard enough to fight boredom, but not too hard as to create anxiety. When "in flow," individuals know exactly what they want to do, feel in control, are immersed in the task, lose their sense of time, are motivated to push themselves further, and receive clear feedback about their performance.

Others can help an employee reach a state of flow by preparing them for the challenge, instilling ways to monitor performance, increasing their focus and confidence, and removing distractions. Helping employees to increase their focus on the present is paramount, so that they can accurately perceive their environment and adapt accordingly.

Behavioral change materializes in organizations in the form of formalized development programs where participants are taken out of their comfort zones and challenged to try new behaviors. On one end of the spectrum are intensive programs where participants go through a series of simulations over three days with a group of their peers and are given behavioral feedback on the spot by a professional coach. After each simulation, the participants are encouraged to reflect on their performance and are given a variety of strategies to try out in the next simulation. Such a program works only when there is a great deal of trust and support, as constant feedback without an up-front coaching contract can be interpreted as a personal attack.

*Action learning* uses the same premise, but strings out the process across several months. In a typical program, participants are challenged to work on a competency, try out new behaviors, get together with a group of their peers, and continue through trial and error until successful change has occurred. On occasion, stretch assignments are given to participants that help to target the specific competency requiring development. Because action learning occurs in small groups, success is dependent on the quality of feedback and advice arising from the group, as well as the chemistry experienced between members.

Recently, I have been involved in the creation of an online development platform that provides structured activities for employees to develop specific behaviors that are appropriate for staff at their level. The activities are supplemented by well-known business models (SWOT analysis for strategy or RACI for planning) in case the participants get stuck. Although I believe that these on-the-job homework assignments have great potential to standardize and encourage meaningful change, they require the involvement of a manager or coach to encourage insight and long-term commitment.

On the other end of the spectrum, organizations can take a passive approach to behavioral change, by simply role modeling competencies. By calling out effective performance or giving *value awards* (medals, plaques, or gift cards), employees are indirectly encouraged to exhibit aligned behaviors. The key is that employees are passively learning what is expected of them by watching how awards and punishments are handed out to others. This stands in stark contrast to the types of learning that occurs through coaching and mentoring, as discussed in the next section.

No matter whether the participant undergoes formal training, simulation, or action learning, the challenge is constrained to one-sided, organizational priorities. Development programs are often a knee-jerk reaction to what is immediately going wrong in the business environment, resulting in a transactional approach to learning. When money is tight, prioritizing development by business need is understandable; however, in the long run and without some allowance for broader, employee-driven development, deterioration in the psychological contract can be expected. Additionally, organizationally driven learning assumes that corporate leaders know exactly what development will drive innovation and continuous improvement in years to come. This is quite an assumption. Who knew that Nokia would transform itself from making paper products to a mobile phone manufacturer.

## Support Through Coaching and Mentoring

As mentioned, strong support structures can ensure that the self-awareness employees gain through assessment and the development challenges they endure lead to long-term change. Other people can provide a sounding board to help participants reflect on what they have learned and to check whether all relevant perspectives were considered. Moreover, supporters can hold participants accountable for their development, encouraging them to reach new levels of proficiency and develop long-term strategies to ensure the investment in time and resources was well spent.

When considering the three forms of development discussed earlier, I believe that organizations can provide support in two distinct ways. When participants are attempting to establish new behavioral habits, *coaching* is the most effective way to ensure that improvement is made. In contrast, if employees are seeking to gain new technical skills or different types of experience, then a *mentor* is more appropriate. The expectations of coaches and mentors differ significantly, yet companies often fail to identify exactly what type of support they require for a particular intervention. We'll start with coaching, which I find to be the more popular of the two.

Organizations embark on coaching programs for a variety of reasons. At the individual level, coaching might be recommended to help an employee through a career transition, deal with a particular workplace challenge, or as a form of remedial action to improve performance. When part of a development program, coaching is used to help assimilate new leaders, ready a talent pool for change, or improve team performance. For the latter, team coaching is sometimes done as a group to address goal setting, roles, systems and procedures, or interpersonal issues.

In reality, very few employees have the opportunity for professional coaching. A survey from 2003 found that 65 percent of organizations used coaches for their top leaders, 58 percent for emerging executives, 48 percent for senior managers, 29 percent for new executives, and 26 percent for mid-level managers, while 26 percent of companies did not use coaching at all. Clearly, coaching is not a form of organizational support enjoyed by the masses.

The one thing about coaching professionals that never fails to amuse me is their affinity for acronyms. It seems that new coaching models spring up on a daily basis. I tend to come across the GROW model the most, which can be used to structure a coaching session by investigating the participant's *Goal*, followed by questioning the *Reality* of the situation, exploring *Options*, and then judging his or her *Will* to take action.

If this acronym doesn't do it for you, you may want to try the PRACTICE model to structure the session (*Problem* identification, *Realistic* goal setting, *Alternative* solutions, *Consider* consequences, *Target* a solution, *Implementation* of *Chosen* solution, *Evaluation*) or maybe the ACHIEVE model (*Assess* the situation, *Creative* brainstorming, *Hone* goals, *Initiate* options, *Evaluate* options, *Valid* action, *Encourage* momentum). Still not doing it for you? How about the POSITIVE model (*Purpose, Observations, Strategy, Insight, Team, Initiate, Value, Encourage*), or the significantly less catchy OSKAR model (*Outcome, Scaling, Know-How, Affirm, Review*).

The acronyms don't stop there, as they are equally prevalent when analyzing specific participant issues. My favorite of this list is the SPACE model, where you define the *Social* context and the impact it has on the participant's *Physical* state, the *Actions* he takes, his *Cognitions*, and his *Emotional* reactions. Alternative models include the less creative acronym of the ABCDE model (*Activating* event, *Beliefs, Consequences, Disputation* of beliefs, and *Effective* approach) or the SCARF model (*Status, Certainty, Autonomy, Relatedness*, and *Fairness*) for predicting whether social interactions will be perceived positively or negatively.

In general, these models define the standards of what a good coaching session looks like. Successful coaching engagements are dependent on a strong relationship between the coach and participant, with strict confidentiality and established boundaries about what is off limits. The coach provides observations to increase the participants' self-awareness, challenging them to think more broadly, take risks, and come up with their own solutions. They might use assessments or background material on the company or the participants' responsibilities to ground the conversation. Throughout the session, the coach establishes and maintains a safe psychological environment that inspires the participant to take action.

A coaching session is not a one-off conversation, but an ongoing process of development. Engagements typically last between three months to a year and a half, with individual sessions ranging from thirty minutes to two hours. Logistics aside, coaching is not something that is done *to* people, but rather a partnership with joint responsibilities. In sessions, the coach and participant should:

- Agree on what is to be accomplished,
- Clarify expectations for the engagements (number and duration),
- Commit to being open and exploring alternate perspectives,
- Engage each other in dialogue,
- Show respect for each other,
- Demonstrate courage and commitment to action, and
- Maintain confidentiality.

Not everyone is cut out to be a coach, which is sometimes forgotten by organizations wishing to sponsor an internal coaching program. The allure of moving to an internal model is understandable, as the cost of hiring external, professional coaches can be hefty. Internal coaching program leaders also argue that their staff can provide a direct link to other development programs, understand the organizational culture, utilize internal expertise, and be resourced more quickly.

For such a program to be successful, sponsors should be aware that their coaches are limited in the types of encounters they can support. After all, most internal coaches have a day job that looks and feels very different from that of a professional coach. Moreover, an internal coach may be unable to challenge the status quo or encourage divergent thinking.

Even with significant training, I am also skeptical about whether internal coaches can provide an objective perspective on a participant's problems. The coach is privy to the internal workings and political landscape of the company, which can taint the coach's understanding of the participant's need. Moreover, intimate knowledge about the participant is now known by a fellow employee of the company. Even with the tightest confidentiality, the coaching relationship may prove to be a conflict of interest.

The International Coaching Federation has created a list of competencies that both internal and external coaches should aspire to. They should maintain ethical standards, establish trust, and form a coaching agreement with the participant. When coaching, they should demonstrate powerful questioning, engage in active listening, and be direct. Their coaching engagements should create awareness, identify actions, and set achievable goals. Finally, they are responsible for maintaining a coaching presence and driving accountability.

Coaches can come from all walks of life. Their qualifications can range from practical business experience as leaders or HR professionals, to clinical or sport psychologists. What ties them together is their interest in helping people improve their work satisfaction and performance, as well as the variety, creativity, and problem solving called for on the job.

Lately, there has been a push to formalize the job of a coach, to clamp down on bad practice and the potential psychological harm done by unqualified individuals. Although there are various accreditations available to check when selecting coaches, registration and licensing is not foolproof, as marginally qualified individuals simply avoid using protected professional titles. Companies are advised to check a coach's background, contact references, and ask for professional qualifications before retaining his or her services. Moreover, because of the highly interactive and personal nature of a coaching engagement, it is essential to judge the level of fit between the coach and participant and to make a change when needed.

The level of fit is also crucial when establishing a mentoring relationship. Unlike coaches, mentors offer their professional experience to guide and role model how a participant might develop. The mentor's strength is in helping employees navigate a career and an organization, rather than providing deep personal insight or changing habits. In considering mentor-participant fit, a recent meta-analysis showed that mentors who share aligned values, display similar workplace attitudes, and come from common professional backgrounds as their participants create more fruitful relationships. Surface similarities, such as age, gender, or ethnicity, had virtually no effect on their effectiveness.

A long-lasting mentoring relationship shares many commonalities with coaching, for example, honoring confidentiality, establishing a safe psychological environment, contracting joint responsibilities, constant engagement, and holding each other accountable for attaining goals. What differs is the content of the conversation and the expectation that the mentor will provide clear advice to the participant. As many mentors come from the same organization as the participant, the insight they can provide around structure, processes, and politics is valuable to less experienced staff.

The Office of Personnel Management issued a guide in 2008 that identified four primary types of mentoring relationships. Mentors can act as *career guides* to steer employees through a profession or company, *information sources* to build knowledge, *intellectual guides* to hone skills, or simply as friends who provide a *sounding board*. This report also discussed the various ways mentoring programs are constructed. To identify the right fit, some companies support "flash mentoring," where participants are shopped around to a variety of mentors, reminiscent of speed dating. Other organizations elect to do group mentoring, where one expert is shared among four participants, or team mentoring, where one participant has access to a panel of experts.

In theory, line managers can act as mentors (termed supervisory mentoring), but I believe that the power of mentoring is in providing support outside normal workplace interactions. The alternative perspective of a mentor, who does not necessarily have to be more advanced in the hierarchy, can legitimize the requests of the participant's manager, identify key skills and experiences required to meet job responsibilities, and demonstrate that there are different ways to advance one's career.

As you can see, mentors and coaches provide different types of support, and both are crucial for ensuring that the knowledge gained by assessment and the investment spent on development challenges result in real change. Yet, the support offered by coaching and mentoring is not immune from the transactional focus identified for both self-awareness and challenge initiatives. For most organizations, coaching and mentoring are reserved for only the most critical staff, working on priorities that are core to the business. It is sometimes offered to staff members as a form of corrective action, above and beyond normal performance management. The masses are left to their own devices.

Due to recent cost-cutting and the resulting shift to using internal coaches and mentors, many are concerned over the extent to which support is truly offered. With an external mentor or coach, participants can openly talk about the barriers, politics, and frustrations affecting their work. With internal resources, some topics are off limits. Likewise, mentors and coaches are not free to speak their minds about the organization or to suggest non-traditional ways to improve the participant's situation. If the participant fails, the reputation of both the participant and supporter is on the line. Because of this, development support that should be building the relational aspects of the psychological contract may fall short of achieving this end.

## Moving Together or Apart

In this chapter, we looked at the ways organizations can encourage greater supplementary fit among their staff by embellishing the goals, values, and norms that are held in common. If employees perceive that their employer is helping them grow in their profession and they are collectively working toward the same ends, employees will typically invest more in the job and keep engaged through organizational change and tough periods. This form of investment reframes the psychological contract as building the non-transactional components of the employment relationship.

However, these benefits are seldom fully realized, as development programs have a tendency to deviate from their intended purposes. Instead of rejuvenating the psychological contract and realigning employees to their workplace, development programs can be subverted by the needs of the organization, which can do harm to the employment relationship. This can happen in all phases of development programs, from building self-awareness to providing opportunities for challenge and organizational support.

One of the clearest ways that development programs go wrong is when the information picked up in assessment, normally intended to raise self-awareness and uncover development needs, is used for purposes beyond the scope of the program. Organizations find it tempting to use readily available information about staff to form their next promotion or appraisal decision. Less often, the real purpose behind development can be to expose poor performers or to decide who to retain when the company goes through restructuring. Having mixed purposes runs contrary to the notion of employee development, where employees are encouraged to identify their weaknesses and try out new ways of working. Using assessment data for any other purpose breaks confidentiality and mutual trust, placing the psychological contract at risk.

A more subtle failure of development programs lies in their content. When companies recognize that change is needed, they often embark on developing staff to fulfill new needs. They train new skills, impart expert knowledge, and model behaviors that they believe are aligned to a revised corporate strategy. This is all very understandable; however, when these initiatives consume the entire development budget and are mandatory, damage is done to the psychological contract. The message is that only organizational priorities matter and that the individual needs of employees to advance in their careers are not valued. The same message is given when an organization identifies strict lanes where development occurs, holding fast to their competency or capability models. Since the psychological contract is based on a reciprocal relationship, reminding employees about the power differential between them and their employer does little to strengthen the bond. Moreover, development that occurs outside a literal translation of the business strategy can result in innovation, creative problem solving, and richer social networks that benefit all.

Both of these failures are evident in the type of support provided by organizations. Coaches and mentors are often briefed about the topics to be discussed during their sessions, as well as defined outcomes that they should achieve. They are sometimes required to report on progress and reveal the extent of the participant's development needs. The implications are even greater for internal coaches and mentors, as the information they gain about a colleague is hard to forget and can be revealed in unintentional ways. Just the fact that an individual has sought support may be perceived as a form of weakness. In true supportive environments, participants are allowed to experiment and fail. I am unsure whether the same holds for the majority of companies sponsoring development programs, where participants are indirectly encouraged to take a cautious approach in what they reveal and which actions they try out.

I believe our job as practitioners is to look after the best interest of both employees and the organizations they serve. Development is a great way to promote a strong employment relationship; yet, to realize its full potential, practitioners need to safeguard the use of personal information, provide open and supportive environments for learning, and balance the power distance between employees and their organizations. We have the potential to set in motion a virtuous cycle where happy and fulfilled talent repay their companies with long-term commitment and performance.

# Chapter 6

## Change

Until this point, we have considered what goes into ensuring a strong and healthy match between employees and their workplace. We have looked at how practitioners gain a deep understanding of what is required on the job and how this is translated into recruitment, assessment, and development initiatives. We have looked at person-environment fit, with its supplemental and complementary components that attach employees to their jobs, managers, teams, and organizations.

We have yet to consider change to the employment relationship. Change can take a variety of shapes and sizes, from a department-wide reshuffle with layoffs to a request by a manager to take on different job responsibilities. Either way, change disrupts the status quo and, depending on the health of the psychological contract, can lead to unintended consequences for the organization.

As varied as the change itself, employees can react differently to the same situation. How optimistic they are, whether they value security, and their age can all affect whether employees welcome change and are likely to accept its consequences. Some individuals crave change in the workplace and, in fact, their psychological contract would be threatened if they didn't experience some sort of change every couple of years.

Change is a necessary part of any healthy organization. To react effectively to consumer preferences or market forces, companies alter how work is performed and who is assigned to it. The reality is that the pace of change has accelerated in recent years. Following the global recession, CEB discovered that 98 percent of companies polled had undergone significant change in the past five years.

Yet, the change does not need to be significant to alter the psychological contract. Subtle change, such as changing the targets someone is held accountable for, steering a staff member toward a critical role, or diverting investment to only high potential staff, can all do damage. Depending on what was promised or conveyed at hiring, these changes have the potential to disrupt the employment relationship.

For example, an employee who learns that he or she is no longer eligible for educational sponsorship due to the establishment of a new high potential program might not only feel dissatisfied with the situation, but feel betrayed. If he or she perceived that sponsorship would be given, even if not explicitly stated, the psychological contract held between that employee and the employer could be irreparably damaged.

This chapter explores how organizations go about changing their cultures, performance standards, and staffing. Many of these change processes have been carefully considered by well-meaning leaders, with clear objectives for transforming how staff are engaged with and managed. Where the process falls down is in the consideration of how these changes are likely to be perceived by employees and whether staff will have to be re-contracted with following the change.

With the minor revolution that has occurred in human resources over the past five years, with an increasingly sophisticated set of tools and processes to manage talent, practitioners have the potential to be even more distracted from considering the employees' vantage point.

The beginning of this chapter will explore the mechanics behind a violation and eventual breach of the psychological contract. This is followed by a discussion about some of the more typical processes used to realign staff to an organizational change, specifically succession planning and performance management. The chapter ends with a consideration of "Big Data" and how technology alters how talent decisions are being made. By focusing overwhelmingly on realigning talent to changes in the business, organizations have a tendency to under-appreciate how change is likely to affect the employment relationship. As practitioners, we have the opportunity to take a broader perspective, advocate for employees, and guide the organization toward a new way of working.

# Breaking the Psychological Contract

When change occurs, the status of the psychological contract held between employees and their workplace is threatened. What may have once been a productive relationship can turn into a performance management intervention or employee resignation, with ramifications that can spill into an employee's immediate workgroup and beyond.

Common to all violations in the psychological contract is a break in the obligations held by either party in the employment relationship. For example, the expectations that an employee has prior to accepting an offer of employment are compared to his or her actual experiences on the job. If these expectations are left unfulfilled, a violation has occurred in the psychological contract and the employee would likely begin looking for an escape plan. It is important to note that the employee's emotional reaction ("Get me out of here") follows the cognitive realization that there is a disconnect between what was promised (perceived or real) and what is being experienced.

Not surprisingly, the focal point for most psychological contract violations is the relationship between the employee and the line manager. Jobs change and, when they do, the line manager is responsible for breaking the bad news. The bad news can take the form of an employee being stripped of a title, reassigned to a new unit, or required to take on new tasks. Managers are usually aware that they are breaking the psychological contracts of their workers, but report that they have little control in the situation. Organizational priorities have shifted, and line managers are left to pick up the pieces.

I have a great deal of sympathy for mid-level managers, as they truly are at the coal-face in delivering difficult news to staff. Few employees recognize that the bad news affecting them has likely resulted in an equally unsettling change for their boss. They, too, may have lost prestige or responsibility in the wake of a change in business strategy.

Violations in psychological contracts are painful to endure. In my career, I have experienced two major changes that have had a lasting impact on me. One violation occurred when I accepted a job that failed to live up to the expectations set by the hiring manager. The second occurred when my team went through a massive reorganization, leaving me with a choice between a place I enjoyed living and a job in a different location. The lack of control over my own destiny and the decrease in self-confidence resulting from these experiences are still with me to this day. I feel somewhat comforted that negative emotions are the norm when it comes to change and that I am not being overly sensitive.

Unsurprisingly, violations are most likely to occur in an already troubled employment relationship. Organizations that have a history of conflict with staff, high social distance between parties, and outside incentives that work against the relationship are prone to violation. When offered a job in a troubled organization, candidates should think twice about whether the environment has truly stabilized or whether the situation is about to return to a more strained time.

The issues most likely to cause friction sit at the most basic level of the employment relationship. Specifically, violations occur most commonly around compensation, promotion, and personal development. Mixed with a poor relationship with management, it is not surprising that these same features are reported by Talent Drain as the top reasons why employees resign.

How any given employee responds to a violation depends on both the type and strength of the psychological contract. Employees holding a predominately relational psychological contract (characterized by feelings of long-term commitment) are generally more resistant to violations. These employees typically voice their concerns and attempt to renegotiate the relationship. If the breach is severe enough, employees may switch into a transactional psychological contract, whereby they weigh up their perceived contribution against the rewards and benefits they receive.

Those already within a transactional mindset are most likely to retaliate against their employers by withdrawing, causing destruction, or exiting completely from the relationship. Incidentally, it is extremely difficult to transform a transactional mindset back into a relational one and therefore, concerted effort should be spent on creating a plan for employees before the violation occurs.

To this end, psychological contracts can be preserved by three primary strategies. First, new responsibilities can be accommodated within the existing relationship. If the change is well communicated (with a clear vision and set of expectations) in an already strong relationship, while the employee is consulted with, reassured, and treated with dignity, a relational psychological contract can be preserved.

Alternatively, managers can hit the reset button and attempt to transform the psychological contract into something completely different. Offering a new job, with a new manager, in a different region is an extreme example (and one that happened to me), but can be an effective way to keep a valued employee when accommodation would be too messy or not in the best interests of the company. Clear guidance should be given to the employee about the need for change, what his or her new role will look like, and an acknowledgement that the old way of working is no longer appropriate. In essence, this is no different from making a fresh hire.

The third strategy really is not a strategy at all. Contract drift occurs when the psychological contract is ignored for a prolonged period. Managers and employees do not actively talk to each other about their expectations and, over time, the relationship takes a different form than where it started. Such an approach can be effective for some organizations, for example, small entrepreneurial companies where staff do a little of everything; however, drift often goes too far, into areas where neither party is prepared to accommodate.

Whether new responsibilities are accommodated, jobs transformed, or psychological contracts left to their own devices, trust is required for any enduring employment relationship. Transparency, consistency, and follow-through go a long way to set up a psychological contract for change.

Organizations go to great lengths planning for change, to minimize the disruption caused to employees and the business. Practitioners use multiple levers to keep the engagement and productivity of employees high through periods of change. In the following sections, we will look at two of the most prominent, succession planning and performance management, before looking at how companies are becoming increasingly obsessed by data and the quest to find a silver bullet to answer all their talent management woes.

## Succession Planning

Smart organizations plan for the future. They worry about their supply chain, product positioning, and brand image. Once they detect a risk to their business strategy, they take immediate action and make an investment. Until recently, human resources would not have ranked high among functions that organizations should be strategic about, but the tides have turned. Without the right people in the right roles, the success of any organization is now recognized as limited.

This is where succession planning comes in. By understanding where the company is headed, the roles required by staff along this journey, and the personal characteristics that will make employees successful, a company can plan for the future and give its strategy a fighting chance.

Despite wide acceptance of the idea that succession planning should be done, there is a feeling among leaders that nobody is doing it well. Research conducted by CEB in 2013 discovered that 82 percent of CEOs are unsure whether they have the right people on board to execute their strategy. Further, 97 percent of respondents stated that they were unaware of where talent resided in their organization. Backing up this concern, it is reported that less than 15 percent of direct reports could comfortably step into their manager's shoes.

When advising clients, I take a structured and pragmatic approach to succession planning. I first ask them to define what their organizational DNA looks like. This can actually be a very difficult task for business leaders, as they tend to rely on organizational charts, rather than what the company is fundamentally tasked to do. For example, a large multinational retailer was able to define its DNA by three strands, those of design, transport, and customer experience. As a second example, a financial services company I worked with concluded that they brought money in, moved it around, and paid claims. Everything else was just a support function.

This task of defining the organizational DNA brings focus to those areas that require succession planning. The bad news for the majority of HR practitioners is that we are not one of those groups. The only exception would be within a consulting practice like the one I work for.

The second task in succession planning is to identify the critical roles that are absolutely required in each of the strands of organizational DNA, both for now and into the future. It is important not to bias people leadership positions above expert contributor roles, as both can be enormously beneficial to the bottom line. Arguably, the technical skills residing with individual contributors are the hardest to replace. Focusing solely on leaders could be disastrous to a company. For example, a key position within any insurance company is the underwriter; however, underwriters seldom lead teams so may be overlooked when doing succession planning. We'll discuss more about this bias for leaders and high potentials shortly.

At this point, we have figured out the roles and functions that require our attention or, put another way, where the demand is for talent. The next step is to define the characteristics required by staff in critical roles. I fall back upon the five key ingredients I outlined in the beginning of this book, specifically, key activities, behaviors, skills, experience, and motivation, to build up a success profile that articulates the role for both now and the near future. This is the benchmark that is used to evaluate bench strength and the priorities for recruitment and development.

Practitioners have a choice about how deep this job analysis should go. I have personally seen effective programs define their characteristics by job families, while others have taken the time to write up success profiles for every critical role. Either way, the content must be clearly articulated at a level that will allow for effective people decisions, taking account of current and future needs.

With our criteria in hand, we are now ready to evaluate the readiness of the talent pool. Any combination of the assessments reviewed in the previous chapters can be included in a talent audit. The quality and extent of the data captured in a talent audit can vary greatly. A study conducted in 2011 found that formalized assessments were used in 52 percent of succession planning programs. This leaves 48 percent of companies that used other means to build a picture of readiness, usually accomplished through manager evaluations.

The data captured helps organizations understand their supply of talent and whether they have enough bench strength to deliver on their strategy. Different slices of the data can be presented, giving a snapshot of readiness for a specific position, a pool of like-skilled individuals who can be deployed readily across positions, or the level of specific skills or expertise available. Talent gaps are often reported as the percentage of roles that have a clear successor or by the ratio of turnover to identified successors.

When displayed visually in a Talent Board like the example provided in Figure 6.1, the information is powerful. Each series of three

| | Finance | Customer Service | Sales |
|---|---|---|---|
| **Director** | | | TW ● ● ● |
| **Mid-Level Manager** | PL ● ● ● | FL ● ● ● | SK JH ● ● ● ● ● ● |
| **Front-Line Leader** | ED WB ● ● ● ● ● ● | MM TU JW ● ● ● ● ● ● ● ● ● | SH AR TT ● ● ● ● ● ● ● ● ● |
| **Individual Contributor** | NJ TJ BR KJ ● ● ● ● ● ● ● ● ● ● ● ● | LL CS MA ● ● ● ● ● ● ● ● ● | GH WW VC VW PJ BH ● ● ● ● ● ● ● ● ● ● ● ● ● ● ● ● ● ● |

FIGURE 6.1   Example of a Talent Board Broken Down by Level and Department

circles represents an individual in a given function, at a specific level. A traffic light system (green, yellow, red) indicates assessment results, such as whether employees have a strong track record of performance, demonstrate alignment to behavioral competencies, and have potential to progress. When a box is dominated by red and yellow (that is, the talent bench is weak), the function may have a succession problem.

By using a visual like this, leaders are instantly able to recognize the sustainability of their business and the likelihood that they have the right people to deliver on their promises. When readiness is mixed with each employee's risk of leaving (either because of retirement or regretted churn), the picture becomes even clearer.

Recently, organizations have begun using talent profiles as a visual way to capture everything about an employee on one sheet of paper. Set up like a baseball card, the employee's work history, education, work interests, skills, performance, and assessment data are displayed for talent managers to discuss and plan around. These talent profiles are an incredible value for organizations, as they move the conversation away from analyzing employees to discussion about where they fit in the organization's strategy and where their careers are likely to go.

All this data analysis without action is pointless. Following any kind of succession planning activity, leaders are charged to do something about the results, both at the employee level and across workgroups. Typical outcomes of a successful talent review include rotating key employees into roles where they have had limited exposure or initiating training on skills that are not currently developed. If either of these strategies is insufficient, external hiring may be the only way to plug a talent gap.

As a real-world example, one of my clients went through a succession planning process of their senior management team, discovering that nearly half of the top leaders were in need of rotation if they were to ever break down organizational boundaries. Working within a single profession (one strand of their DNA) was fine under their previous organizational structure, but would be disastrous following their recent transition from a public to a private entity.

To evaluate the effectiveness of the succession planning process, practitioners will often turn to metrics such as the number of vacancies currently open, number of people ready to move up, the ratio of internal to external hires, or the attainment of new skills. If set up correctly, with a clear focus on the roles that are imperative to execute the business strategy, succession planning can add huge value to the organization.

How often organizations should go through this process is a matter of debate. I generally advise clients to minimize the burden to the business (both for employees going through assessment and for talent review committees to discuss the results) by either rotating which divisions go through the process during a given year, resetting the process on a two-year cycle, or simply waiting for a dramatic change in strategy to identify when it is appropriate to complete a full-scale review of talent.

## High Potentials and the Learning Agile

In the last section, I made an assumption that succession planning is grounded by the identification of critical roles that carry a high degree of risk if left vacant or filled with the wrong talent. However, most organizations do not view talent this way and are more interested in identifying a broad pool of high potentials who can be tapped to fill any number of leadership roles. Before we go into the benefits and drawbacks of this approach, let's examine exactly what is meant by "high potential."

The CEB high potential model, first published in 2005, provides an excellent shorthand for defining the attributes of employees who are most capable of taking on more responsibility or complexity in their jobs. High potentials are said to possess the ability (thinking agility to work through more strategic or complicated issues), aspiration (desire for leadership roles and the willingness to exert extra effort to get there), and engagement (identifying with and feeling energized by their work). By definition, a high potential employee must have ample amounts of ability, aspiration, and engagement.

This is only half the story. Before we even look at any employee's potential for more complicated work or higher levels of responsibility, he or she must be a strong performer in the current job. Performance is not the same as potential and, in fact, the majority of strong performers in an organization will never be considered as high potentials. CEB looked at the combination of performance and potential, discovering that only 29 percent of high performing employees were also considered high potentials (that is, employees sitting within the top quartile of both performance and potential). The remaining 71 percent of high performers were likely to struggle or fail if promoted.

A common way to represent the combination of potential and performance is the nine-box grid shown in Figure 6.2. This graphic is a quick means of distinguishing those individuals who are likely to benefit from accelerated development and more intensive career management.

As shown, each box has its own descriptor of the type of individual falling within it. Organizations invest in the top right-hand boxes, labeled here as High Potentials and Solid Potentials. These individuals show great promise in their ability and ambition (potential), while having at least proven competence (if not mastery) within their current roles.

When we look more in-depth as to why not all high performers are high potentials, the necessity for having ability, aspiration, and engagement become clear. Employees with aspiration and engagement, but deficiency in ability, are called Engaged Dreamers and have no chance of being successful at a higher level. CEB estimates that 10 percent of high performers who are not high potentials fall into this category. Employees with ability and engagement, but who lack

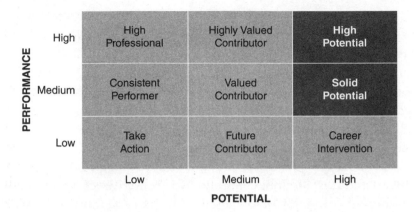

FIGURE **6.2** Example of a Nine-Box Grid of Performance and Potential

aspiration to take on more responsibility, are called Misaligned Stars. These employees make up 47 percent of high performers who are not high potentials and have a fairly good chance at being successful in a higher role, at 44 percent. These employees are your solid performers who are happy doing what they are doing. They would benefit from career enrichment, rather than promotion.

The last category is made up of employees with ability and aspiration, but who lack engagement with their current employer. These Unengaged Stars make up 43 percent of high performers who are not high potentials and have little chance of being successful at a higher role, at 13 percent. Under normal circumstances, these employees would be good candidates for investment, but without addressing their engagement to the company, any promotion or development would be unlikely to turn things around. They are high potential, but perhaps not for your organization.

Embarrassingly, I once made the mistake of trying to promote an Unengaged Star. The consultant I worked with was extremely talented and definitely able to do more than what she was currently doing. I saw ability and aspiration in spades, but also knew that she was growing tired of her job and the company. Trying to be proactive, I promoted her and gave her a bump in salary, just in time for her to negotiate for a new role with a different employer. It was a great lesson that ability and aspiration are not enough in evaluating who should be prioritized in succession planning.

We are about to enter a very interesting labor market. If we believe the engagement research, Unengaged Stars have grown in number since the financial crisis. CEB found a 48 percent drop in the number of high potentials between 2005 and 2010. The cause of this drop was not the aspiration or ability of employees, but rather their engagement. In comparison with the average employee, high potentials have experienced more layoffs of team members, significant restructuring, and changes in job responsibilities.

As companies attempt to do more with less, high potentials have suffered and now are looking around for better career opportunities. Considering that high potentials are 91 percent more valuable to an organization, these are not the employees you want to disenfranchise. When the labor market becomes more buoyant, it will be interesting to see how many companies are successful at retaining their high potentials.

A related concept is learning agility. In 2000, Lombardo and Eichinger proposed that learning agile employees actively seek out learning experiences, enjoy complex problems they have not encountered before, gain a great deal from working out puzzles, and generally perform better due to the quick uptake of new skills.

Learning agile employees are able to gain new skills and to hone existing ones in order to perform well in unfamiliar contexts. They avoid derailment by identifying a need to try out a new problem-solving strategy. Using this model as a guide, Korn Ferry has created tools to measure the four components of learning agility, specifically People Agility, Results Agility, Reward Agility, and Change Agility.

The Center for Creative Leadership agrees on the importance of learning agility. In 2012, they defined the learning agile as being more extroverted (sociable, active, and likely to take charge), original (creates new plans, seeks complexity, and accepts change), less accommodating (challenges others, welcomes engagement, and expresses opinions), resilient (calm, optimistic, and rebounds from failure), and focused (organized, driven, and methodical). They, too, offer assessments for learning agility, reporting back on employees' tendencies for innovating, reflecting, risking, performing, and defending (this last trait is not desirable in the model).

Both high potentials and the learning agile are said to benefit from a safe psychological environment, with abundant learning opportunities, the right amount of career challenge, and support from mentors and role models. They require the freedom to experiment and the time to consolidate their learning for future use.

This sounds reasonable on the surface; however, I wonder why these guidelines are not suggested for everyone. Beyond purely egalitarian aims, investing only in high potentials or the learning agile assumes that we can correctly identify the right employees to take part in accelerated learning. A large number of the clients I interact with on a daily basis are still relying on subjective ratings by managers to identify who is high potential. These are the same people providing performance ratings, so it is hard to imagine their ratings of potential will be anything different from what they have already ascribed for performance.

Although a step in the right direction, many of the tools on the market touted to correctly identify potential rely on questionnaires (either self-reports or manager feedback) or, alternatively, utilize structured interview questions. As noted earlier, subjectivity can creep into any of these assessments and, because of the high stakes inherent with labeling only a small percentage of employees as high potential, great care should be given before buying into one of these tools in isolation. Even harder to swallow is a sole reliance on cognitive ability as a measure of potential, for the same reasons expressed earlier when discussing general intelligence.

Beyond issues of identification, positioning what it means to be high potential is a minefield. The general rule of thumb among practitioners is that transparency around high potential programs should be an aspiration. The type of training employees receive, the prospects of future positions, and the requirements to join the program should be considered and communicated to all interested staff. A fair and consistent application or nomination process should be implemented. Personally, I favor a stepped approach whereby a consistent track record of strong performance in the current role is a prerequisite for being recognized as a high potential for future roles.

A mixture of manager nomination, objective measurement of fit to leadership roles, and a conversation with the employees to gage their current level of aspiration seems to strike the right balance. If someone passes these criteria, then accelerated development might be a viable strategy for talent managers to invest resources on those most likely to contribute to the organization.

Three conditions must be met for me to be comfortable with designating a high potential group of employees. First, the designation should be time dependent, a snapshot of a particular employee and a workplace at a specific moment in time. The requirements of the job, relationships with managers, career aspirations, and organizational engagement are in constant flux and, therefore, no employee can be excluded from being considered to have potential when the next review occurs. This view is in conflict with that of many of my peers, who view learning agility or potential as a trait, inherent to an employee and unlikely to change over time.

Second, employees who fail to attain the designation of high potential or learning agile should continue to be valued by the organization. Development, learning opportunities, and support should be offered widely in a company and not just to employees sitting at the highest box in the nine-box grid. Forgetting the 90 percent of employees sitting outside this designation would be disastrous for any organization.

Last, a designation of high potential or learning agile should not guarantee placement into a leadership role when one becomes available. As with any other selection decision, a fair and equitable process should be followed whereby the talents of each applicant are weighed against the role requirements. Just because a candidate is deemed to have potential does not mean that he or she is ready to take on a leadership role or greater job complexity.

If any of these three conditions is broken, the psychological contract across employees is in jeopardy. Those who apply for high potential programs, but fail to gain a spot, will feel dejected if it means they are blocked from future leadership positions. Likewise, organizations that guarantee development only to the lucky few convey to everyone else that the employment relationship is temporary and transactional in nature. I would like to say that the majority of companies manage their high potential programs well, but, in reality, I believe that they are doing more harm than good by disenfranchising the larger workforce.

## Driving Performance

Among the topics discussed in this book, performance management is probably one of the most accepted talent management practices. It is up there with hiring and firing, covering the middle ground of keeping employees focused on the job. Yet, there is a great deal of controversy about what performance management means and which are the most effective activities.

In the last two years, we have witnessed massive investment in performance management systems. With SAP buying Success Factors and IBM purchasing Kenexa, the systems that capture and compile employee ratings have hit the big league. Companies have taken notice and want to change up how they drive employee performance. Brian Kropp wrote in 2013 that 86 percent of companies polled were either in the process of changing their performance management systems or planning to do so in the near future.

The reason for this emphasis on performance management systems stems from the massive change organizations have undergone following the economic downturn. CEB reported that, from 2008 to 2012, close to 98 percent of companies had experienced considerable change and, although CEOs had hoped otherwise, only 60 percent have hit their new performance targets.

Fueling this fire is discontent among HR executives about the quality of data being captured in their performance management processes. In a recent poll, only 23 percent of human resource directors believe that their systems accurately reflect the contributions of their employees.

In general, the maximum benefit that a well-applied system can achieve is a 5 percent improvement in performance. This is not an inconsequential number and can mean millions of dollars for larger organizations. However, most organizations are held accountable for much higher growth targets, and performance management can only make up a fraction of the overall plan to grow a business.

Hidden in the overall success rate is a great deal of diversity in how performance management practices are applied. Kropp noted that, of the 300 companies he researched, there was no appreciable difference in the performance achieved by a company based on the type of process it adopted. This does not mean that we are lacking some universal principles, but rather that the way in which those principles are applied does not matter much.

Until recently, there was a high degree of agreement about the elements of an effective performance management system. Across any given year, a formal appraisal would occur to review the previous year's performance, highlighting personal contributions and areas in which expectations were left unfulfilled. Managers ascribe a score that, when rolled up and calibrated within a work group, results in a pay increase or promotion.

After a short period of time, a development conversation occurs, wherein the employee and manager reflect on the appraisal and complete an individual development plan (IDP) to set the expectations for the coming year. The goals identified are meant to be SMART (Specific, Measurable, Actionable, Realistic, and Time Bound) and focused on areas that have the greatest potential to drive the business. Although there is the opportunity to talk about development that is purely for the individual, the emphasis is on identifying ways to increase performance.

As a means of elevating this planning discussion, assessments might be introduced to raise the awareness of the employee. By using personality or motivation instruments, participants gain a perspective on areas that they naturally gravitate to and that, therefore, provide an understanding of why some areas consistently turn up as developmental needs. Research from 2011 suggests that 47 percent of companies use formalized assessments somewhere in the performance management process.

If not used in the first development conversation, they are likely used at the half-year review, when progress to date is evaluated against IDP goals. 360-degree feedback falls naturally into these conversations, as employees can track what parts of their behavior have had the biggest impact on those around them. The last part of the cycle ends as it began, with a formal appraisal.

Over the past decade, a variety of ideas have been touted as best practice for organizations implementing performance management. First, large scale IT platforms have been set to work capturing the objectives and ratings made about employees. Second, cascading goals attempt to link each individual's targets to the overall business strategy of the company. Last, e-learning and development tips are suggested for individuals based on their needs.

However, despite the best of intentions, much of this advice does not matter. In regard to large data systems, the technology itself is not bad, but its use changes how we approach the activities. What we work on, when we do it, and how we approach our development is dictated by the architects of the performance management system. Whether or not a development module is easily accessible may make the difference on what we do, regardless of whether the development will have an impact on our performance.

For example, if competencies are hard set into the system, this might restrict or discourage development that sits outside of these parameters. One performance management system I personally experienced was organized by organizational values. Although I appreciate that the designers of our system were trying to encourage a common culture, I had immense problems trying to shoehorn my development needs into one of those buckets. Moreover, the deadlines set for updating information did not coincide with when my development needs became apparent, nor when I wanted to work on them. Instead of helping me set goals that would facilitate my development, the process became a burden and solely a record of what I did.

A related concern is the relevance of cascading goals. It is extremely difficult to track the relationship between any individual's job and the overarching goals of a company. Someone in the research and development department in a telecommunications company may only have a very tentative relationship to something like customer service. They might define peers in other departments as internal customers to make their development fit with a cascading goal, but I doubt that this was the original intent of why a company would take on customer service as a strategic priority. Moreover, it may be very difficult for someone in a department like R&D to set time-bound objectives, if the results of their work span multiple years or have a long ramp-up period.

In the 2011 *Society for Human Resource Management Handbook*, the myths of performance management were exposed, with the goal of truly identifying what best practice should be. Contrary to popular belief, performance management data is not required for pay or promotion decisions. The data captured can actually do more harm than good, as it is often not differentiated enough to justify decisions, nor consistent in how it is captured, rated, and normalized. Moreover, the documentation it provides can actually impede a specific reward or disciplinary decision, as it often does not provide the detail required to justify such talent decisions.

The true best practice suggested by the handbook includes providing relevant feedback informally and in real time. Managers should convey what the individual is doing right or wrong, using clear criteria for expectations and tangible examples of performance shortly after the actual occurrence. Development should be talked about on the spot, with growth opportunities identified and tied back to the criteria.

This best practice allows for plenty of space for assessment and development activities, but does not assume that they will be directly tied to what is seen on the job. As mentioned earlier in the book, assessments can effectively raise one's self-insight, while overarching development goals can encourage staff to improve. The practice puts the emphasis back on performance as witnessed on the job and improves relevance and chances for corrective action. The one drawback to the new best practice is that it places a huge amount of responsibility on managers, who may be ill-equipped to pay close attention and offer strong advice.

Beyond these lofty goals, the SHRM handbook outlines the legal requirements of any process. Practitioners should ensure that only relevant factors of a job are evaluated, inform staff of performance expectations, document what the process involves, train managers on what they need to do, require managers to record performance and complete all elements of the process, review ratings for inconsistency and bias, and have an appeal process in place.

From what I have seen, performance management is at a crossroads. There is massive investment occurring to allow for an enterprise-wide implementation across large numbers of employees. Yet, many of these systems are like the "emperor with no clothes." All the features are in place, but content and substance are lacking.

As it is currently implemented, performance management does a poor job of rejuvenating the psychological contract and promoting change within a workforce. When the system doesn't seem relevant, is disconnected from on-the-job activities, and lacks developmental insight, the amount of time and resources spent on performance management appear wasteful. Worse, if performance management is used to aggressively promote an organizational change (that is, more difficult targets), there might not be enough positive feedback, development, and investment identified in the process to energize and motivate staff.

# Big Data and Monitoring Change

With the advent of readily available information about virtually everything an employee does, ranging from customer interactions and sales to unofficial web browsing, it is not surprising that leaders are data mining to find what's happening in their business. The problem is that, without knowing what to look for or how good the quality of the data is, the process can be fruitless. They might actually find something that does not exist (referred to as a Type 1 error in statistics) just because they conducted so many analyzes.

The notion of setting metrics makes sense and can help focus staff on what matters most. The Balanced Scorecard (Kaplan & Norton, 1996) has been around for a while and provides a framework to expand the conversation beyond purely financial indicators. Kaplan and Norton outline six areas to monitor within a company, including:

- *Financial metrics:* cost, revenue, profit, return, and growth
- *Innovation:* new products, patents, and inventions
- *People:* retention, satisfaction, and engagement
- *Process:* operational efficiency, resource consumption, and quality
- *Customer:* acquisition, satisfaction, retention, and market share
- *Community:* media attention, reputation, and corporate social responsibility

Many of the these metrics have been monitored and acted upon for years. They are the foundation for board reports and investment decisions. Yet, only in the last five years has momentum grown around the *people* component. For example, Bersin reports that in 2011, nearly one-half of companies surveyed utilize a ninety-day new hire assessment to gage quality of hire.

Aberdeen Group in 2010 found that the top five metrics used by companies include manager satisfaction with hire, employee performance, workplace engagement, retention rate, and level of staff vacancies. Other people metrics have lagged behind. For example, a CEB study found that, despite 80 percent of practitioners stating that they believed applicant reactions to the hiring process were important, only 36 percent of companies actually captured this information.

To track all this data, companies have invested in and continue to pour money into a variety of technology platforms that serve up HR metrics. A poll of HR leaders found that two-thirds of companies utilize some sort of applicant tracking system for recruitment, with a similar percent using a learning management system for development and a performance management system to drive productivity. Just over half of companies utilize an HR information system that records employee details, while less than half own a system tailored to talent management.

Driving this investment in time and resources is the industry's belief that data will make companies more profitable. For example, Hay stated that companies that adhere to best practice in talent management can expect to perform eight times better in shareholder return. Likewise, the Institute of Personnel and Development reports that 29 percent of the variation in productivity is due to people management, which has a greater impact than strategy, technology, or research and development. Other commonly quoted benefits include lower attrition, higher engagement, and greater advocating on the company's behalf.

The catch is that there is increasing evidence that there is no one best way of driving performance. In a study of credit unions, Drogan and Yancey discovered no relationship between best practice (conducting job analysis, assessment, structured interviews, résumé screening, and validation) and financial performance. Rather, it was establishing the relevance and alignment of these practices to the organization's purpose that was critical.

Brian Kropp commented on a study of 300 companies that there was no significant difference in actual performance due to the type of performance management system put in place by a company. Rather, the underlying philosophy of reward, recognition, and feedback was most important. This is quite a statement considering that the study found that 85 percent of companies are changing or planning to change their performance management systems in the near future.

It appears that Big Data alone will not be the silver bullet organizations hope it will be. Without knowing what data to mine or how to apply it, the effort looks like a fool's errand. Worse, Big Data can be a significant distraction from focusing on the quality of conversations between managers and employees. By switching systems and criteria, the message becomes blurred for employees and apathy can set in, undermining the whole goal of raising performance.

## From a Balanced to a Transactional Contract

In the discussion above, some of the most well-known approaches for dealing with change were explored. By conducting succession planning, establishing a high potential development program, or embedding performance management into everyday activities, companies attempt to realign their staff to a new organizational strategy that is a reaction to changes in the consumer market.

This is what business leaders are tasked to do. Their job is to create sustainable, profitable businesses. Although they inherently know that positive change will fail without the support of employees, leaders under-appreciate the extent to which they are bound to their employees by the psychological contract.

Like any other contract, unilateral change without the involvement or consideration of the other party can lead to a breakdown in trust and dissolution of the relationship. Without clearly understanding what employees value in the relationship or how they are likely to react when the terms of the contract change, leaders make the assumption that their staff will obediently follow along.

A contract does not exist when there is only one participant, so practitioners should advise leaders to take into account the broader implications of change. For example, before initiating a new succession planning process that can lock out staff from promotion, assigning sales staff a new book of business, or changing targets in the performance management system, the implications of change should be considered.

A virtuous feedback process might be a solution. Before the strategy is set in stone and wide-scale change occurs, information about the capabilities and motivations of staff must be considered and fed back to those individuals initiating the change. If the feedback leads to the conclusion that the strategy is impractical due to lack of capability or is untenable from the employees' perspective, then adjustments should be made.

As practitioners, we have an obligation to look after the whole of the employment relationship and not just what the organization requires. Forcing change on employees can work in the short term, but will not lead to a sustainable relationship in the end. We should help organizational leaders step into the employees' shoes when considering change. This can be incredibly difficult when a company is losing money or under immense time pressure; however, without winning employee support, any change in strategy is unlikely to succeed.

If we are effective at representing both parties in the employment relationship, our own relevance and impact are likely to benefit. We will become the brokers of change and have a seat at some of the best conversations taking place in the company. We can aid leaders in quantifying the risk involved in changing strategies, based on how well employees are likely to react, as well as suggest strategies based on the capabilities of current talent.

We have great potential with our shiny new Big Data toolbox, if we learn how to use it effectively. We have only scratched the surface of how we can help business leaders understand their talent and devise a really great strategy. Once we learn how to do this well, we will be a lot closer to ensuring employees have a voice and will be working toward preserving the psychological contract.

# Conclusion

The previous chapters took us on a tour of how people decisions are typically made in the workplace. As we have seen, a diverse and extensive range of tools and techniques can be utilized. Some of these are worthy of use and application across the organization. Others, despite promises to the contrary, can actually do a great deal of harm to the employment relationship.

Alongside this toolbox is organizational inertia, which has to be overcome to ensure that any change in how people decisions are made is sustainable in the long run. Without constant attention and updating, organizations revert to shortcuts and biases that undermine the thoughtful architecture that has been put in place to manage talent. In general, we are currently in a state of misplaced talent, where employees most capable of doing the job are overlooked, not given the resources to grow, and placed in positions that do not maximize their talents.

How we got to this situation is a result of a combination of factors. The most obvious is that we have emphasized the legal elements of talent decisions while failing to either sell the benefits of our approaches or communicate the risk of doing nothing. Compounding this issue, those of us working in human resources, occupational psychology, or other related fields are generally not the best at selling our profession. We often hesitate when talking about business metrics, which makes it difficult for us to be taken seriously and establish equal footing with those working in fields like operations or finance.

Yet, there is potential to set the story straight. Like never before, leaders are interested in data about talent and are hungry for approaches that will help them grow their businesses. There is broad recognition that companies can do more to manage their talent effectively, similar to what was witnessed in supply chain management or quality control in decades past. The stage is set for us to demonstrate what we can do. If we are able to rekindle our passion, reengage business leaders, and demonstrate why investing in better talent decisions matters, there is no doubt in my mind that companies and employees alike will benefit from our efforts.

I hope that you found this book a helpful resource for having more meaningful conversations about how to manage talent in your own organization. To this end, I would like to leave you with a few fundamental concepts. These concepts have provided me with a way to organize my thoughts about the interaction between employees and their workplace. They have also provided me with a shorthand way to quickly express what is of primary interest to the companies I advise.

The term *psychological contract* was introduced as a way of expressing the shared understanding held between an individual and his or her employer about the obligations that are the basis for their relationship. The psychological contract can take a variety of forms, from the transactional to the relational, but what matters is whether both parties understand what is required of them, deliver on their obligations, and trust that these will be fulfilled in the future. Clearly defining the type of contract held by employees and heightening the transparency between parties should be of primary concern for practitioners.

The term *person-environment fit* provides a way of expressing the quality of the employment relationship. Fit is strongest when organizations are able to apply the knowledge, skills, and abilities held by employees, fulfill the tangible and intangible needs of their staff, and help employees believe that they are contributing toward a common purpose. There is much for us as practitioners to do to improve fit. Diagnosing what employees need to possess in order to do their jobs effectively, ensuring that staff use their talents, encouraging companies to provide work environments conducive to employee motivation, and finding a shared purpose that is clearly conveyed across the organization, all make for a very tall order.

When we look at the components around which fit can be established, I commonly refer to the five ingredients of the employment relationship, specifically the *key activities* an employee is typically tasked to complete, the *behavioral competencies* that define how effective employees go about their jobs, the *skills* that enable performance, the *experience* that can be applied to a given context, and the *motivation* that will drive action. By understanding what is required or provided with a given role and how well matched this is

| | Assessment | Development | Support |
|---|---|---|---|
| **Key Activities** | • Performance Indicators | | |
| **Behavior** | • 360 Feedback<br>• Simulations<br>• Competency Interviews | • On-the-Job Practice<br>• Games and Simulations<br>• Action Learning | • Coaching |
| **Experience** | • Resume / CV<br>• References<br>• Biographical Inverviews | • Rotation<br>• Job Assignment | • Mentoring |
| **Skills** | • Ability Tests<br>• Skills Tests<br>• Certifications | • Training<br>• Formal Education<br>• Self-Study | • Instruction |
| **Motivation** | • Personality Questionnaires<br>• Motivation Questionnaires<br>• Values Questionnaires | | |

FIGURE **7.1** Summary of How to Assess, Develop, and Support Staff

to an employee, fit can be predicted and action taken by employers to maintain the psychological contract.

Across these five ingredients, different types of assessments can be used to evaluate fit or raise *self-awareness*. They give rise to different forms of *development challenge* and *organizational support* (the three components of employee development). In the table provided in Figure 7.1, I have listed some of the most prevalent ways of assessing, developing, and supporting employees. As can be seen, assessment occurs across all five ingredients; however, development and support are restricted to behavioral competencies, skills, and experiences. Key activities are defined by what is required from an individual and, although new targets can be set, it would be difficult to call this development. Also, motivations are inherent to the employee. Companies can change the work environment to match an employee's motivations, but this does not count as development.

I hope I have encouraged you to think about people decisions in a new way. Potentially, you, too, will embark on a critical evaluation of how well you truly understand the drives and desires of those around you, as well as whether you are providing the best possible advice to organizational leaders. Along the way, I hope you have gained a few helpful insights.

For my part, the act of writing this book has forever altered the way I think about people decisions. It has reinvigorated my interest in my field and provided a way to consolidate my thinking. I hope that I remember to look back in a few years to see whether we have made any progress and have successfully found our talent.

# About the Author

**Joe Ungemah, D.Occ.Psych.,** is a practitioner at heart. As a consultancy practice leader and registered psychologist, he spends his days sharing with his clients the techniques that result in better people decisions and more satisfied employees. His skill is in translating the complex field of occupational psychology into simple and straightforward advice. After studying and working on three continents, he is now based in Minneapolis, Minnesota. Visit his website at www.workpersona.com.

# Acknowledgments

A project like this requires the support of a great number of people. Beyond recognizing the pleasure of working alongside some of the best practitioners and clients around, as well as Matt Davis and the Wiley team for believing in this book, I would like to thank my parents for teaching me how to work, my brother for showing me what a true role model looks like, my children for providing an opportunity to laugh every day, and especially my wife, who will always be my strongest collaborator and best friend.

# Resources

## Chapter 1

For more information on the history and modern uses of job analysis, see:

Mitchell, J. (1988). History of job analysis in military organizations. In S. Gael (Ed.), *The Job Analysis Handbook for Business, Industry and Government* (1, 30–36). Hoboken, NJ: John Wiley & Sons.

Singh, P. (2008). Job analysis for a changing workplace. *Human Resource Management Review, 18,* 8–99.

Wilson, M. (2014). A history of job analysis. In L. Koppes (Ed.), *Historical Perspectives in Industrial and Organizational Psychology* (219–241). Mahwah, NJ: Lawrence Erlbaum Associates.

Below are a couple of links to take advantage of publicly available resources:

Competency Clearinghouse: www.careeronestop.org/CompetencyModel/

O*Net: www.onetcenter.org/

Specific resources referenced when talking about competency models, career paths, and job evaluation include:

Boyatzis, R. (1982). *The Competent Manager: A Model for Effective Performance.* New York: John Wiley & Sons.

Carter, G., Cook, K., and Dorsey, D. (2009). *Career Paths: Charting Courses to Success for Organizations and their Employees.* Hoboken, NJ: John Wiley & Sons.

Hay Group. (2014, June). *Job Evaluation: Foundations and Applications.* Philadelphia, PA: Author.

*IRS Employment Review.* (2006). Competency Benchmarking Report. Washington, DC: IRS.

Woodruffe, C. (1992). What is meant by a competency? In R. Boam and P. Sparrow (Eds.), *Designing and Achieving Competency.* Maidenhead, UK: McGraw-Hill.

## Chapter 2

Main sources about top companies to work for include:

Gersch, K. (2013, August 21). Google' s Best New Innovation: Rules Around "20% Time." *Forbes.*

Glassdoor. (2014). Employees' Choice Awards Results: www.glassdoor.com/

Great Place to Work. Survey Background and 2014 Results: www.greatplacetowork.com/

Mims, C. (2013, August 16). Google Effectively Kills "20 Percent Time," the Perk That Gave Us Gmail. *Huffington Post.*

Universum. (2014). U.S. Student Survey Results: www.universumglobal.com/

# Sources consulted in writing about EVP and employer brand include:

Ambler, T., and Barrow, S. (1996). The employer brand. *Journal of Brand Management, 4,* 185–206.

Bersin and Associates. (2011). *The Talent Acquisition Factbook.* Oakland, CA: Author.

CEB. (2014). *Benchmarking the Employment Branding Function.* Arlington VA: Author.

Deloitte. (2014, October): http://mycareer.deloitte.com/au/en/life-at-deloitte/ouremployeevalueproposition

Garibaldi, A. (2014). *Employer Branding for Dummies: Glassdoor* (special ed.). Hoboken, NJ: John Wiley & Sons.

Hill, B., and Tande, C. (2006). *Total Rewards: The Employment Value Proposition.* Scottsdale, AZ: WorldatWork.

LaMotte, S. (2014, October 6). Job Seekers Aren't Stupid, so Start Being Honest with Them. *Forbes.*

Mokina, S. (2014). Pace and role of employer brand in the structure of corporate brand. *Economics and Sociology, 7,* 136–148.

O' Keefe, R. (2014). How EGC Could Become Your EVP (TMP white paper). New York: TMP.

Schmidt, Lars. (2013, June 20). Amplify Talent, This Is NPR Recruiting: An Employment Branding Case Study. (blog post)

Schmidt, Lars. (2013, December 30). Amplify Talent, The Anatomy of a Top 10 LinkedIn Company Page: Inside NPR. (blog post)

Schmidt, Lars. (2014, March 4). Amplify Talent, Introducing: The Brand Recruiting Twitter List. (blog post)

Schmidt, Lars. (2014, September 15). Amplify Talent, A Case for Reinventing Job Descriptions (blog post)

SHRM. (2008). *The Employer Brand: A Strategic Tool to Attract, Recruit and Retain Talent.* Alexandria, VA: Author.

Smedstad, Shannon. (2014, March 10). Blogging4Jobs, #1 Thing You Need to Know About Employer Branding. (blog post)

Smedstad, Shannon. (2014, July 28). Blogging4Jobs, Candidates Are Hungry: Is Your Recruitment Marketing Snackable? (blog post)

Smedstad, Shannon. (2013, August 5). Blogging4Jobs, How Corporate Recruiters Play a Key Role in Your Employer Brand. (blog post)

Smedstad, Shannon. (2014, August 11). Blogging4Jobs. Are Your Employees Positively Amplifying Your Brand? (blog post)

Towers Watson. (2012). *Employer Value Proposition: Key to Getting and Keeping the Best.* New York, NY: Author.

Universum. (2014, October): http://universumglobal.com/2014/03/what-is-employer-branding

## Chapter 3

Regarding the research on dishonesty, below are the main studies referenced:

- The first study was conducted by Galaxy research on behalf of SHL Australia in May 2010, with data collection occurring between the 4th and 7th of May. One thousand ten Australians aged eighteen and over who had been for a job interview in the last two years were polled. Approximately 200 interviews were conducted in each state, and the total was weighted to reflect national demographics.
- The second study about impact on the brand was conducted by SHL and included in the 2012 Business Outcomes Study Report.
- A third study is mentioned in a SHL white paper from 2006, titled Better Practice for Unsupervised Online Assessment.

Specific references on the history, power, and prevalence of assessments include:

Aberdeen Group. (2010). *Talent Assessment Strategies*. Boston, MA: Author.

Avery, R., and Campion, J. (1982). The employment interview: A summary and review of recent research. *Personnel Psychology, 35,* 281–322.

Cable, D., Higgins, C., and Judge, T. (2000). The employment interview: Recent research and recommendations for future research. *Human Resource Management Review, 10,* 383–406.

Chartered Institute of Personnel and Development. (2004). *Recruitment, Retention and Turnover*. London, UK: Author.

Hoffman, B.J., Melchers, K.G., Blair, C.A., Kleinmann, M., and Ladd, R.T. (2011). Exercises and dimensions are the currency of assessment centers. *Personnel Psychology, 64,* 351–395.

Huffcutt, A., and Arthur, W. (1994). Hunter and Hunter (1984) revisited: Interview validity for entry-level jobs. *Journal of Applied Psychology, 79,* 184–190.

Ifould, R. (2009, March 6). Acting on impulse. *The Guardian.*

Kleinmann, M., Ingold, P.V., Lievens, F., Jansen, A., Melchers, K.G., and König, C.J. (2011). A different look at why selection procedures work: The role of candidates' ability to identify criteria. *Organizational Psychology Review, 1,* 128–146.

Mischel, W., and Peake, P. (1982). Beyond deja vu in the search for cross-situational consistency. *Psychological Review, 89,* 730–755.

Newcomb, T. (1929). *The Consistency of Certain Extrovert-Introvert Behavior Patterns in 51 Problem Boys*. New York, NY: Columbia University Teachers College.

Robertson, I., and Smith, M. (2001). Personnel selection. *Journal of Occupational and Organizational Psychology, 74,* 441–472.

Shackelton, V., and Newell, S. (1991). Management selection: A comparative survey of methods used in top British and French companies. *Journal of Occupational Psychology, 64,* 23–36.

SHL. (2009–2014). *Global Assessment Trends Reports.* Arlington, VA: Author.

UK Government, Employers' Manpower and Skills Practices Survey (1990–1991).

Below is the information referenced on legal requirements:

Australian Legislation: www.fairwork.gov.au/about-us/legislation

Myors, B. (2006). International perspectives on the legal environment for selection. *Industrial and Organizational Psychology, 1,* 206–246.

Specific references cited when discussing IQ include:

AFL-CIO PayWatch website post (2001, April 5). http://htp.workingamerica.org/Press-Room/Press-Releases/AFL-CIO-PayWatch-Website-and-New-E-Campaign-Turns

Ericsson, A., Krampe, R., and Tesch-Romer, C. (1993). The role of deliberate practice in the acquisition of expert performance. *Psychological Review, 3,* 363–406.

Gardner, H. (1983). *Frames of Mind.* New York, NY: Perseus.

Gladwell, M. (2008). *Outliers.* New York, NY: Penguin.

Gould, S. (1996). *The Mismeasure of Man.* New York, NY: W.W. Norton.

Murdoch, S. (2009). *IQ.* London, UK: Wiley.

Sternberg, R. (1997). *Successful Intelligence.* New York:, NY Penguin.

# Chapter 4

For more information on the topic of motivation, see:

Deci, E., and Ryan, R. (2000). The "what" and "why" of goal pursuits: Human needs and the self-determination of behavior. *Psychological Inquiry, 11,* 227–268.

Forer, B. (1949). The fallacy of personal validation: A classroom demonstration of gullibility. *Journal of Abnormal and Social Psychology, 44,* 118–123.

Herzberg, F. (1968, January/February). One more time: How do you motivate employees? *Harvard Business Review,* pp. 53–62.

Latham, G. (2007). *Work Motivation.* Thousand Oaks, CA: Sage.

Maslow, A. (1943). A theory of human motivation. *Psychological Review, 50,* 370–396.

McGregor, D. (1957). The human side of enterprise in adventures in thought and action. *Proceedings of the Fifth Anniversary Convocation of the School of Industrial Management.* Cambridge, MA: MIT.

Pinder, C. (1998). *Work Motivation in Organizational Behavior.* Upper Saddle River, NJ: Prentice Hall.

Pinder, C. (1984). *Work Motivation.* Glenview, IL: Scott, Foresman and Company.

Pink, D. (2011). *Drive.* New York, NY: Penguin.

RedBalloon. (2009, November). Reward and Recognition Survey. Sydney, AU: Author

Schneider, B. (1987). The people make the place. *Personnel Psychology, 40,* 47–453.

Schneider, B., Goldstein, H., and Smith, D. (1995). The ASA framework: An update. *Personnel Psychology, 48,* 747–773.

Sheldon, W. (1954). *Atlas of Men*. New York, NY: Harper.

Talent Drain. (2008). Employee Retention Survey. www.orghealth.co.uk/uploads/ articles/Employee%20Retention%20Survey%202008%20-%20Dispelling%20 the%20Myths%20Surrounding%20Retention.pdf

Van Eerde, W., and Thierry, H. (1996). Vroom's expectancy models and work-related criteria: A meta-analysis. *Journal of Applied Psychology, 81*, 575–586.

Warr, P. (1986). A vitamin model of jobs and mental health (pp. 157–164). In G. Debus and H. Schroiffs (Eds.), *The Psychology of Work and Organization*. North Holland, The Netherlands: Elsevier Science Publishers B.V.

Warr, P. (2007). *Work, Happiness, and Unhappiness*. Mahwah, NJ: Lawrence Erlbaum Associates.

Sources speaking more directly to aging and generational effects include:

Cherrington, D., Condie, S., and England, J. (1979). Age and work values. *Academy of Management Journal, 22*, 617–623.

Goldberg, E. (2005). *The Wisdom Paradox*. London, UK: Free Press.

Howe, N., and Strauss, W. (2008, July/August). The next 20 years: How customer and workforce attitudes will evolve. *Harvard Business Review*, pp. 41–52.

Kanfer, R., and Ackerman, P. (2004). Aging, adult development, and work motivation. *Academy of Management Review, 29*, 440–458.

Li-Ping Tang, T., and Yann Tzeng, J. (1991). Demographic correlates of the Protestant work ethic. *The Journal of Psychology, 126*, 163–170.

NAS Insights. (2006). Generation Y: The Millennials. www.nasrecruitment.com/uploads/files/recruiting-managing-the-generations-04-2014-90.pdf]

Rhodes, S. (1983). Age-related differences in work attitudes and behavior: A review and conceptual analysis. *Psychological Bulletin, 93*, 328–367.

Smola, K., and Sutton, C. (2002). Generational differences: Revisiting generational work values for the new millennium. *Journal of Organizational Behaviour, 23*, 363, 382.

Twenge, J. (2006). *Generation Me*. New York, NY: The Free Press.

Wentworth, D., and Chell, R. (1997). American college students and the Protestant work ethic. *The Journal of Social Psychology, 137*, 284–296.

Links to the psychometric instruments and governing bodies are provided here:

British Psychological Society: www.bps.org.uk

Minnesota Multiphasic Personality Inventory: www.pearsonclinical.com/

California Personality Inventory: www.cpp.com

Occupational Personality Inventory and MFS 360: www.shl.com/us

Myers Briggs Type Indicator: www.cpp.com

16PF: www.pearsonclinical.com/

Below are specific references about employee engagement:

Becker, T., Billings, R., Eveleth, D., and Gilbert, N. (1996). Foci and bases of employee commitment: Implications for job performance. *Academy of Management Journal, 39*, 464–482.

Chartered Institute of Personnel and Development. (2007). *Reflections on Employee Engagement: Summary of Results from the 2006 Ipsos Mori poll.* www.cipd.co.uk/hr-resources/research/employee-engagement-reflections.aspx]

Eby, L., Freeman, D., Rush, M., and Lance, C. (1999). Motivational bases of affective organizational commitment: A partial test of an integrative theoretical model. *Journal of Occupational and Organizational Psychology, 72,* 463–483.

Grant, A. (1997). Relational job design and the motivation to make a pro-social difference. *Academy of Management Review, 32,* 393–417.

Harter, J., Schmidt, F., and Hayes, T. (2002). Business-unit-level relationship between employee satisfaction, employee engagement, and business outcomes: A meta-analysis. *Journal of Applied Psychology, 87,* 208–279.

Hay Group. (2001). *Engage Employees and Boost Performance.* Philadelphia, PA: Author.

Judge, T., Thoresen, C., Bono, J., and Patton, G. (2001). The job satisfaction–job performance relationship: A qualitative and quantitative review. *Psychological Bulletin, 127,* 376–407.

Nix, G., Ryan, R., Manly, J., and Deci, E. (1999). Revitalization through self-regulation: The effects of autonomous and controlled motivation on happiness and vitality. *Journal of Experimental Social Psychology, 35,* 266–284.

UCEA. (2010). *The Business Case for Wellbeing and Engagement: Literature Review (captures, among other research, the Watson Wyatt study from 2009).* www.ucea.ac.uk/download.cfm/docid/09029336-65F2-44CA-B53631B5E111DFCA

Wegge, J., Schmidt, K., Parkes, C., and Van Dick, R. (2007). Taking a sickie: Job satisfaction and job involvement as interactive predictors of absenteeism in a public organization. *Journal of Occupational and Organizational Psychology, 80,* 77–89.

# Chapter 5

Main sources about trends in learning and development include:

American Society for Training and Development (2013). *State of the Industry.* Alexandria, VA: Author.

CEB. (2001). *Voice of the Leader.* Arlington, VA: Author.

CEB. (2003). *Maximizing Returns on Professional Executive Coaching.* Arlington, VA: Author.

CEB. (2009). *Unlocking the Value of On-the-Job Learning.* Arlington, VA: Author.

SHL. (2009–2014). *Global Assessment Trends Reports.* http://ceb.shl.com/us/forms/content/gatr

For more information on the psychological contract, see:

Arnold, J. (1996). The psychological contract: A concept in need of closer scrutiny. *European Journal of Work and Organizational Psychology, 5,* 511–520.

Herriot, P., Manning, W., and Kidd, J. (1997). The content of the psychological contract. *British Journal of Management, 8,* 151–162.

McFarlane Shore, L., and Tetrick, L. (1994). The psychological contract as an explanatory framework in the employment relationship (pp. 91–109). In C. Cooper and D. Rousseau (Eds.), *Trends in Organizational Behavior*. Hoboken, NJ: John Wiley & Sons.

Millward, L., and Brewerton, P. (2000). Psychological contracts: Employee relations for the twenty-first century (pp. 1–53). In C. Cooper and I. Robertson (Eds.), *International Review of Industrial and Organizational Psychology*. Hoboken, NJ: John Wiley & Sons.

Millward, L., and Hopkins, L. (1998). Psychological contracts, organizational and job commitment. *Journal of Applied Social Psychology, 28*, 1530–1556.

Millward-Purvis, L., and Cropley, M. (2003). Psychological contracting: Processes of contract formation during interviews between nannies and their "employers." *Journal of Occupational and Organizational Psychology, 76*, 213–241.

Rousseau, D. (2004). Psychological contracts in the workplace: Understanding the ties that motivate. *Academy of Management Executive, 18*, 120–127.

Rousseau, D. (1995). *Psychological Contracts in Organizations*. London, UK: Sage.

Schein, E. (1980). *Organizational Psychology*. Englewood Cliffs, NJ: Prentice Hall.

Sutton, G., and Griffin, M. (2004). Integrating expectations, experiences, and psychological contract violations: A longitudinal study of new professionals. *Journal of Occupational and Organizational Psychology, 77*, 493–514.

## Sources about differences in self-insight and feedback seeking include:

Ashford, S., and Tsui, A. (1991). Self-regulation for managerial effectiveness: The role of active feedback seeking. *Academy of Management Journal, 34*, 251–280.

Bracken, D. (1994, September). Straight talk about multi-rater feedback. *Training and Development*, pp. 44–51.

Fedor, D., Rensvold, R., and Adams, S. (1992). An investigation of factors expected to affect feedback seeking: A longitudinal field study. *Personnel Psychology, 45*, 779–805.

Garavan, T., Marley, M., and Flynn, M. (1997). 360 degree feedback: Its role in employee development. *Journal of Management Development, 16*, 134–147.

Korman, A. (1976, January). Hypothesis of work behavior revisited and an extension. *Academy of Management Review*, pp, 50–63.

London, M., and Smither, J. (1995). Can multi-source feedback change perceptions of goal accomplishment, self-evaluations, and performance-related outcomes? Theory-based applications and directions for research. *Personnel Psychology, 48*, 803–839.

Roberson, L., Deitch, E., Brief, A., and Block, C. (2003). Stereotype threat and feedback seeking in the workplace. *Journal of Vocational Behavior, 62*, 176–188.

Tuckey, M., Brewer, N., and Williamson, P. (2002). The influence of motives and goal orientation on feedback seeking. *Journal of Occupational and Organizational Psychology, 75*, 195–216.

Williams, J., Miller, C., Steelman, L., and Levy, P. (1999). Increasing feedback seeking in public contexts: It takes two (or more) to tango. *Journal of Applied Psychology, 84*, 969–976.

Below are references that speak about experience, coaching, and learning:

Csikszentmihalyi, M. (1975). *Beyond boredom and anxiety*. San Francisco, CA: Jossey-Bass.

Ericsson, A., Krampe, R., and Tesch-Romer, C. (1993). The role of deliberate practice in the acquisition of expert performance. *Psychological Review, 3,* 363–406.

Fitts, P., and Posner, M. (1967). *Human Performance*. Belmont, CA: Brooks/Cole.

Gordon Training International. (2014). *Learning a New Skill Is Easier Said Than Done* (for Noel Burch's original learning model). West Solana Beach, CA: Author.

International Coach Federation: www.coachfederation.org/

McCall, M.W., Jr., and Hollenbeck, G.P. (2002). *Developing Global Executives*. Boston, MA: Harvard Business School Press.

U.S. Office of Personnel Management (2014). *Best Practices: Mentoring*. Washington, DC: Author.

## Chapter 6

Main resources consulted when discussing change and trends in performance management include:

Aberdeen Group. (2010). *Talent Assessment Strategies*. Boston, MA: Author.

Bersin and Associates, (2011). *The Talent Acquisition Factbook*. Oakland, CA: Author.

CEB (2010). *Improving Returns on Leadership Investments*. Arlington, VA: Author.

CEB. (2013). *Driving Breakthrough Performance in the New Work Environment*. Arlington, VA: Author.

CEB (2013). *The Analytics Era: Transforming HR's Impact on the Business*. Arlington, VA: Author.

Drogan, O., and Yancey, G. (2011). Financial utility of best employee selection practices at organizational level of performance. *The Psychologist-Manager Journal, 14,* 52–69.

HayGroup. (2009). *Tackling Talent Management*. Philadelphia, PA: Author.

Institute of Personnel and Development. (1998). *Impact of People Management Practices on Business Performance*. http://citeseerx.ist.psu.edu/viewdoc/download?doi=10.1.1.198.2194&rep=rep1&type=pdf

Kaplan, R., and Norton, D. (1996). *The Balanced Scorecard: Translating Strategy into Action*. Boston, MA: Harvard Business School Press.

SHL. (2009–2014). *Global Assessment Trends Reports*. Arlington, VA: Author.

SHRM. (2012). *Building a High-Performance Culture: A Fresh Look at Performance Management*. Alexandria, VA: Author.

For more information on violations to the psychological contract, see:

Coyle-Shapiro, J., and Kessler, I. (2000). Consequences of the psychological contract for the employment relationship: A large scale study. *Journal of Management Studies, 37,* 903–930.

Herriot, P., and Pemberton, C. (1996). Facilitating new deals. *Human Resource Management Journal, 7*, 45–56.

Kropp, B. (2013, November 25). CEB: Is the Performance Management System Dead or Creating Zombies? (blog post)

Millward, L., and Brewerton, P. (2000). Psychological contracts: Employee relations for the twenty-first century (p. 1–53). In C. Cooper and I. Robertson (Eds.), *International Review of Industrial and Organizational Psychology.* Hoboken, NJ: John Wiley & Sons.

Resources that speak about high potentials and the learning agile include:

CEB. (2005). *Realizing the Full Potential of Rising Talent.* Arlington, VA: Author.

CEB. (2010). *The Disengaged Star.* Arlington, VA: Author.

Center for Creative Leadership. (2014). *Learning About Learning Agility.* Greensboro, NC: Author.

Korn Ferry International. (2014). *viaEDGE Learning Agility Assessment.* Los Angeles, CA: Author.

Lombardo, M., and Eichinger, R. (2000). High potentials as high learners. *Human Resource Management, 39,* 321–330.

# Index

Page references followed by *fig* indicate an illustrated figure.